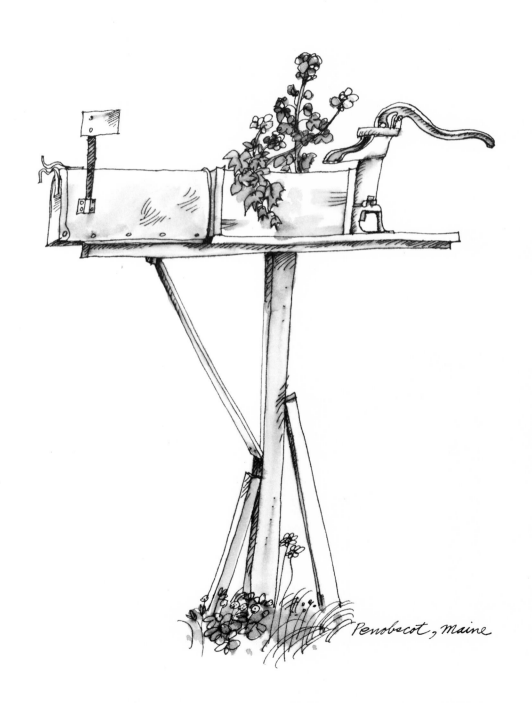

Penobscot, Maine

near Dennysville, Maine

Back Roads of New England

BY EARL THOLLANDER

Clarkson N. Potter, Inc./Publisher   NEW YORK
DISTRIBUTED BY CROWN PUBLISHERS, INC.

Published simultaneously in Canada by General Publishing Company Limited
Inquiries should be addressed to Clarkson N. Potter, Inc., 419 Park Avenue South, New York, N.Y. 10016.
FIRST EDITION

to my wife,
janet

Contents

Hazen's Bird House
Westford, Connecticut

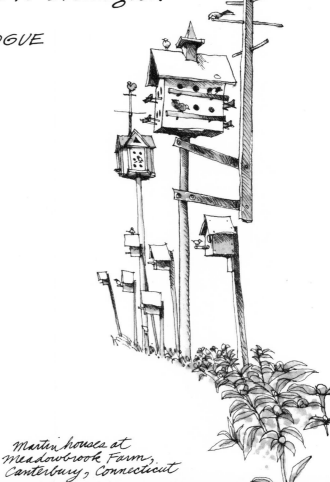

Martin houses at
Meadowbrook Farm,
Canterbury, Connecticut

Greene Herb Gardens,
Greene, Rhode Island.

Preface

This book is an on-the-spot pictorial record of the villages and places I have seen and enjoyed while traveling the back roads of New England. It would be a monumental task to catalog all the delightful back roads in New England. My book is a selection from these roads, a somewhat circular tour beginning in Rhode Island and ending in Maine.

I have not really attempted to outline a tour of New England but rather to inspire you toward your own route selections and back roads adventures. I would suggest that when you wish to go from town to town, and since back roads maps are scarce, ask locally about roads other than normal highway routes. (Get it down on paper, too, so you can't get lost!) That way you may discover a different, more "earthy" New England.

My pace for travel on the back roads ranged from five to thirty miles per hour. This brought me into closer contact with the countryside, for at these speeds I could easily stop to view a scene or talk with someone. At the outset of my travels I stopped to ask a fisherman at a back roads bridge the name of the small tree that was blooming profusely in the area. He said, "That must be the shadbush." He then added with a friendly smile, "Would you like some fish?" I accepted and later enjoyed fresh trout for lunch. The beauty of the shadbush in bloom and the friendliness of a lone fisherman got my travels on the back roads of New England off to a memorable beginning.

Shadbush

Author's note

The six sections of this book all begin with a state map showing the back road areas and associated towns. Official state maps, available free from Travel Services, Chambers of Commerce, Tourist Bureaus, Automobile Clubs, and other sources will direct you to these areas. My local maps should then guide you successfully along the back roads. If you get lost, hopefully you will find yourself on an even more interesting route.

Rather than writing detailed driving directions on how to get onto each back road I have put as much information as possible into the local maps. Distances, village names, road names, when designated (not many were posted in Vermont, New Hampshire, and Maine), nearby highways, and other helpful hints are on the maps themselves. The thicker map line is the back road trip recommended, the arrow is in the direction I traveled (which certainly could be reversed if you were so located) and the North Pole, as it is traditionally indicated, is toward the top of the page. Maps are not to scale due to the diversity in length of many of the roads; however mileage notations have been made where they seem necessary. Useful to me in discovering the back roads of New England were maps furnished by the highway department of each state. The scale used was one inch to the mile which meant that for Massachusetts alone I had to deal with an unwieldy ninety nine maps, each measuring 13½ × 18 inches!

Map Legend		
————	my backroads route	
———	other roads	
··········	more primitive roads	
▲ 3m ▲	distances between points in miles	
— — — —	boundaries of lakes, ponds and rivers	

Rhode Island

    Of the six New England states
Rhode Island is the only one small enough
to be able to show back roads with sufficient
clarity on their official state highway map.
This is a great boon for the inquisitive traveler.
The Rhode Island coast is quite interesting and
popular, however my travels carried me also to the
rural villages, farms, and forests of the state.
    It may be surprising to strangers to
Rhode Island that this tiny state has such
beauty along its interior back roads.

True Forget-me-not

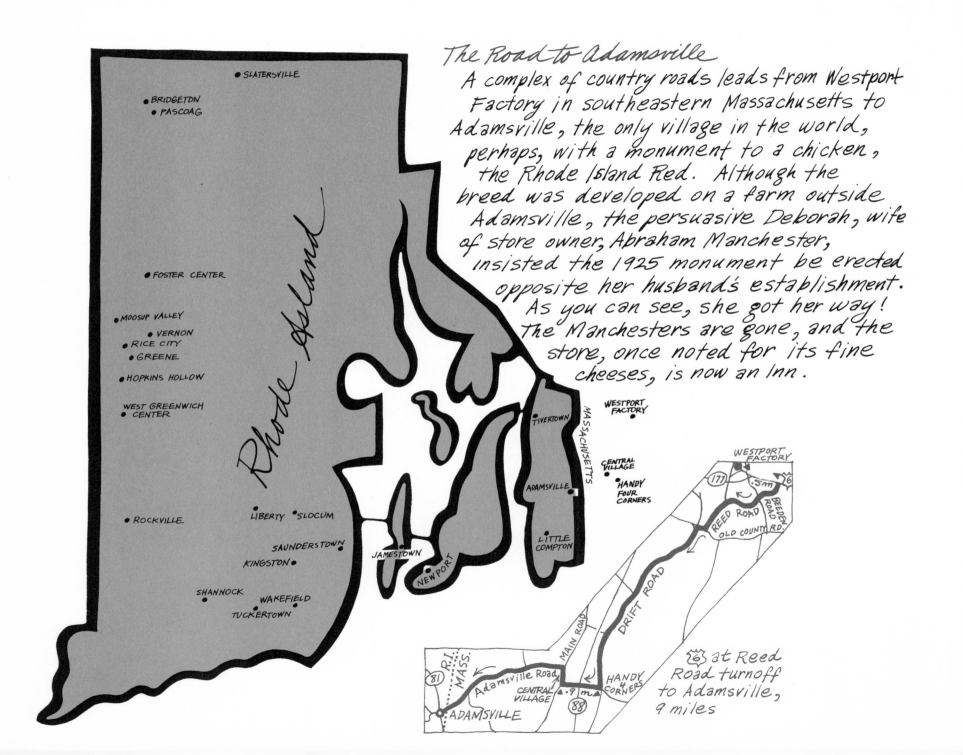

The Road to Adamsville

A complex of country roads leads from Westport Factory in southeastern Massachusetts to Adamsville, the only village in the world, perhaps, with a monument to a chicken, the Rhode Island Red. Although the breed was developed on a farm outside Adamsville, the persuasive Deborah, wife of store owner, Abraham Manchester, insisted the 1925 monument be erected opposite her husband's establishment. As you can see, she got her way! The Manchesters are gone, and the store, once noted for its fine cheeses, is now an Inn.

Adamsville, Rhode Island

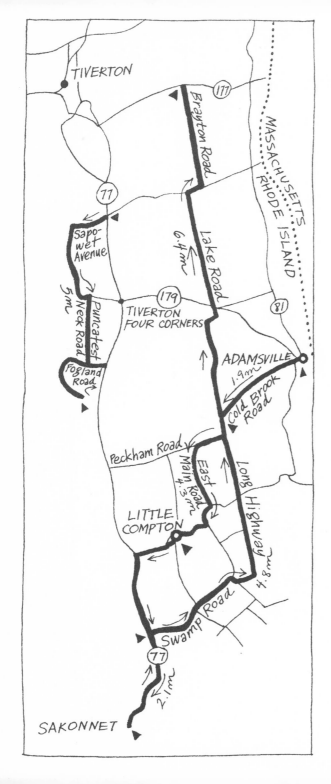

TIVERTON

177

MASSACHUSETTS
RHODE ISLAND

Brayton Road

77

6.4m

Lake Road

Sapo-
wet
Avenue

179

TIVERTON
FOUR CORNERS

81

5m

Puncatest Neck Road

Fogland Road

ADAMSVILLE

1.9m

Cold Brook Road

Peckham Road

East Main Road

Long Highway

4.3m

LITTLE
COMPTON

4.8m

Swamp Road

77

2.1m

SAKONNET

Roads to Little Compton and Tiverton

Impressive are the long walls of stone along these roads, carefully fitted together without mortar. They look as if they will stand forever. On Fogland Road I drew a wall. The setting sun was on my back, warming me against the crisp sea breeze.

Stone wall, Fogland Road

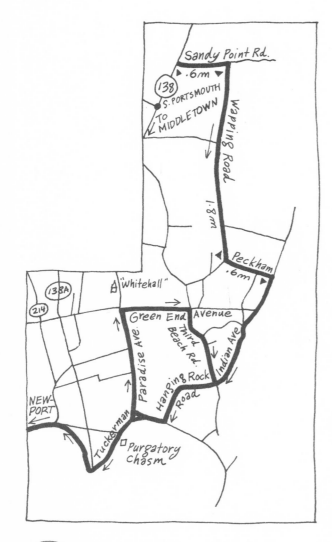

Sandy Point Rd.

▶ .6m ◀

138
S. PORTSMOUTH

TO
↙ MIDDLETOWN

Wapping Road

1.8m

◀ Peckham
.6m ▶

"Whitehall"

138A

214

Green End Avenue

Third Beach Rd.

Paradise Ave.

Indian Ave.

Hanging Rock Road

NEW-
PORT

Tuckerman

□ Purgatory
Chasm

138 at Sandy Point Road, Indian Avenue
to Newport, 8 miles
Paradise Avenue, Green End and
Third Beach Road, 2.3 miles

Indian Avenue to Hanging
Rock and Purgatory Chasm
The stone, vine-covered
St. Columba's Chapel sits
picturesquely in the graveyard
along Indian Avenue. Massive
trees shade the unusually
handsome gravestones and
well-clipped lawn. I admired
the exquisite lettering of a
master stone-cutter on many
of the monuments.

St. Columba's Chapel, Middletown

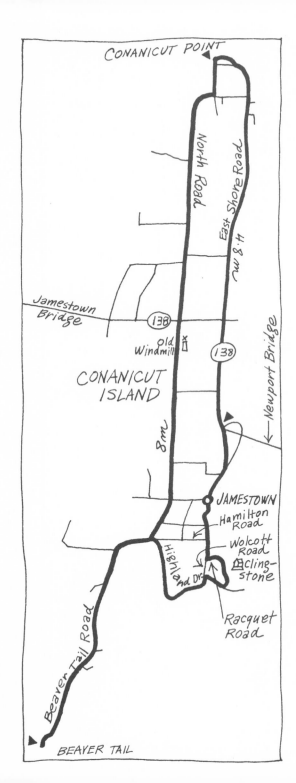

Conanicut Point to Beaver Tail

   It is exciting to see the sea crashing ashore at Beaver Tail during a full storm, I was told. There is also the ancient windmill to view along the way, as noted on the map.

   Built on a rock in Jamestown Harbor around the turn of the century is the unusual and aptly named, "Clingstone House."

Clingstone House, Jamestown Harbor

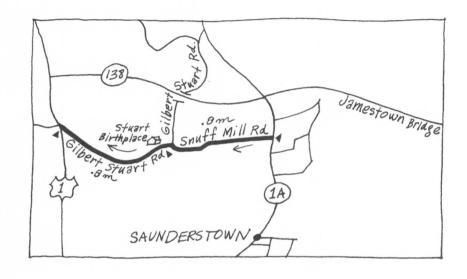

Roads to Gilbert Stuart Birthplace and Snuff Mill

In 1753 the first snuff mill in New England was erected by Gilbert Stuart's father at the head of the Mattatucket River near Saunderstown. Here, in 1755, Stuart was born, to become in later years the most distinguished of American portraitists, particularly because of his portraits of George Washington.

Buttercups

Birthplace of Gilbert Stuart near Saunderstown

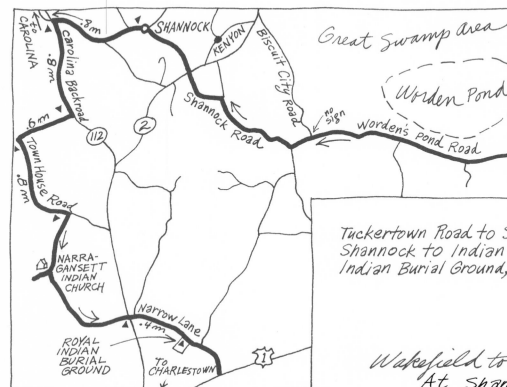

Tuckertown Road to Shannock, 7.2 miles
Shannock to Indian Church and
Indian Burial Ground, 6.4 miles

Wakefield to Tinkertown and Shannock

At Shannock cows ambled down the road and across the bridge over the Pawcatuck River. Some boys came canoeing from Worden Pond, stopped to see what I was drawing, and then portaged around the horseshoe falls. In 1870 this was a mill town with S.P. Clark manufacturing cotton warps and George Weeden making plaid linsey. Today, except for the roar of the falls it seems a quiet, country village.

Horseshoe falls, Pawcatuck River, Shannock

INDIAN CHURCH

1859

Narragansett Indian Church, Indian Cedar Swamp

Shannock to Indian Church and
  Royal Burying Grounds
            The forest surrounded
  Narragansett Indian Church. Peering in the
  window I noticed that the attendance
    roster at the last service was "8".
    There was a small pipe organ and a
  pot-bellied stove in the middle of the room.
    I made my drawing from the meadow in front
    of the church and at one point almost
  dropped my pen as five motorcyclists came
  roaring past me out of the woods shattering
  the profound silence of the place.

Brambles

Across Rhode Island on the Back Roads

All that remains standing in West Greenwich Center is the Town Meeting House, dating from 1750. Northward along the road toward Hopkins Hollow, is the old Tillinghast property. I sat in the meadow and drew the red barn. On the left, under the trees, is one of seven cemeteries on the present 1500-acre property, which is privately owned. There were several Tillinghasts buried here, behind the barn, the latest grave marked 1903.

Long ago this same area consisted of 27 farms, testimony to the fact that this part of Rhode Island, as indeed, all of New England, was once the province of the small farmer.

Now, forests grow between many of the old stone walls instead of crops.

The old Tillinghast barn, near Greene

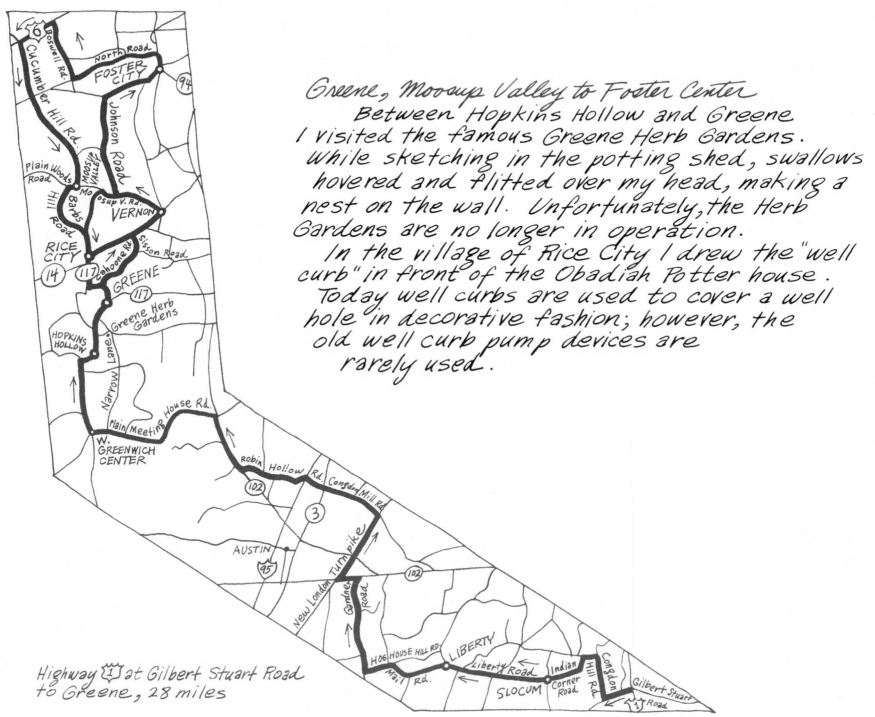

Greene, Moosup Valley to Foster Center

   Between Hopkins Hollow and Greene
I visited the famous Greene Herb Gardens.
While sketching in the potting shed, swallows
hovered and flitted over my head, making a
nest on the wall. Unfortunately, the Herb
Gardens are no longer in operation.
   In the village of Rice City I drew the "well
curb" in front of the Obadiah Potter house.
Today well curbs are used to cover a well
hole in decorative fashion; however, the
old well curb pump devices are
   rarely used.

Highway 1 at Gilbert Stuart Road
to Greene, 28 miles

YEARS MATURE INTO FRUIT SO THAT SOME SMALL SEEDS OF MOMENTS MAY OUTLIVE THEM   TAGORE

WORMS at work
Making Soil

NoThing Leaves the Land

For Goodness Sake plant Comfrey near your Compost

Greene Herb Gardens potting shed, Greene

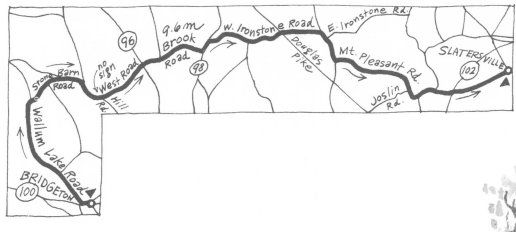

Back Roads to Slatersville

Mt. Pleasant country road leads past the Hutnak barn. Eighty-one-year-old Mr. Hutnak, who is Czechoslovakian-born, admitted to me that the old barn needed fixing but had good, strong, heavy timber inside. I asked him if he knew when it was constructed. He answered, smiling: "I don't know, maybe Columbus built it."

Farm on Mt. Pleasant Road near Slatersville

Well curb, Obadiah Potter House, 1804, Rice City.

Connecticut

It is interesting to see along the way the many millponds of Connecticut and imagine the picturesque waterwheels that once turned in the streams. They varied in size from those of big cotton mills to the waterwheel of a single-owner farm.

Almost every road in the areas of Connecticut explored in the following pages led to historic places, pleasant villages, and friendly people.

Wild Lily of the Valley

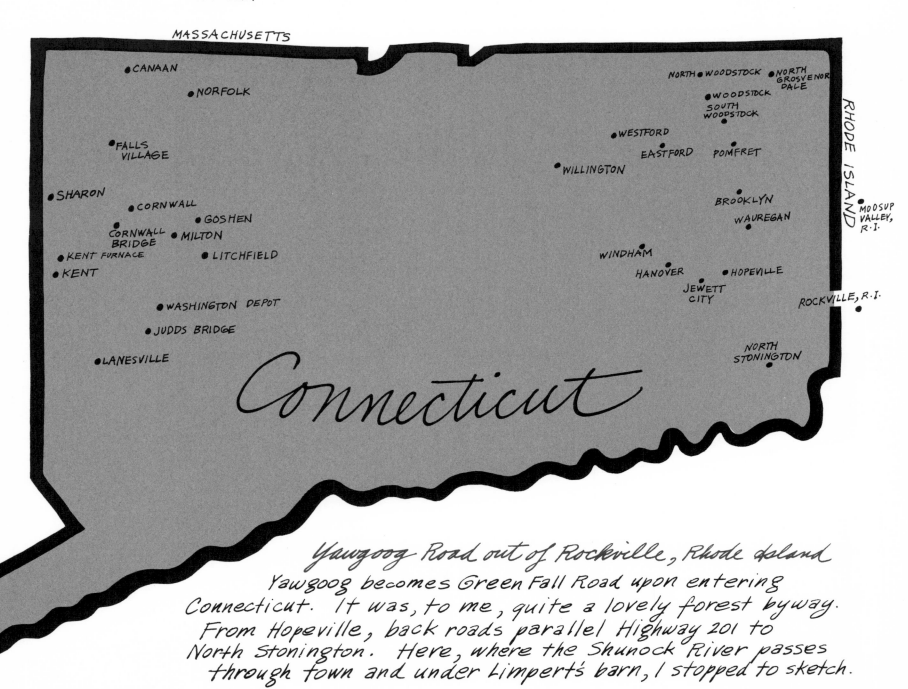

• MONTEREY

MASSACHUSETTS

CANAAN

NORFOLK

NORTH • WOODSTOCK • NORTH GROSVENOR DALE

• WOODSTOCK

SOUTH WOODSTOCK

FALLS VILLAGE

• WESTFORD

EASTFORD   POMFRET

• WILLINGTON

SHARON

CORNWALL

GOSHEN

CORNWALL BRIDGE • MILTON

BROOKLYN

WAUREGAN

RHODE ISLAND

MOOSUP VALLEY, R.I.

KENT FURNACE

KENT

LITCHFIELD

WINDHAM

HANOVER   • HOPEVILLE

JEWETT CITY

ROCKVILLE, R.I.

WASHINGTON DEPOT

JUDDS BRIDGE

LANESVILLE

NORTH STONINGTON

Connecticut

Yawgoog Road out of Rockville, Rhode Island
Yawgoog becomes Green Fall Road upon entering
Connecticut. It was, to me, quite a lovely forest byway.
From Hopeville, back roads parallel Highway 201 to
North Stonington. Here, where the Shunock River passes
through town and under Limpert's barn, I stopped to sketch.

Shunock River, North Stonington

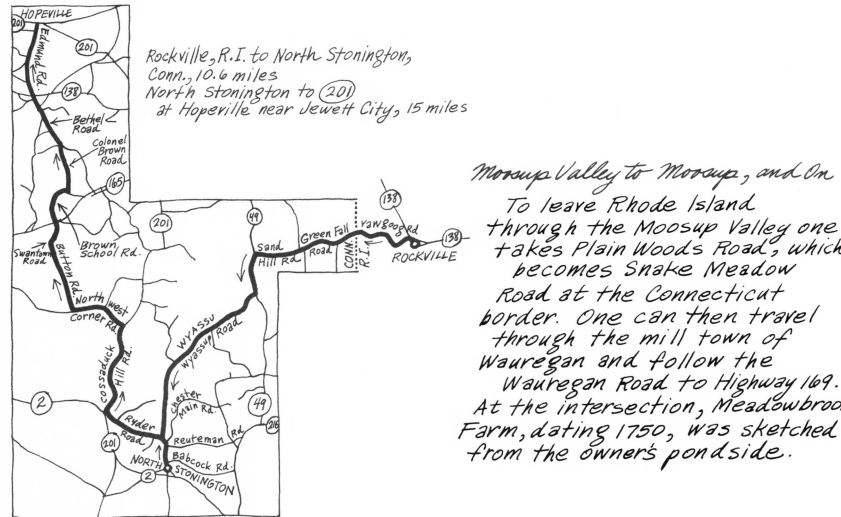

Rockville, R.I. to North Stonington,
Conn., 10.6 miles
North Stonington to (201)
at Hopeville near Jewett City, 15 miles

Moosup Valley to Moosup, and On

To leave Rhode Island
through the Moosup Valley one
takes Plain Woods Road, which
becomes Snake Meadow
Road at the Connecticut
border. One can then travel
through the mill town of
Wauregan and follow the
Wauregan Road to Highway 169.
At the intersection, Meadowbrook
Farm, dating 1750, was sketched
from the owner's pondside.

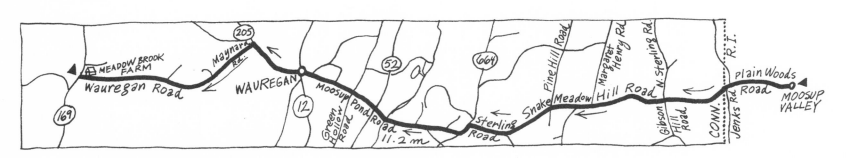

Meadowbrook Farm, Canterbury

Wedgewood Mill, Jewett City.

Stetson Corner to Jewett City

These back roads led to Jewett City and a drawing in town of the old Slater Mill to the accompaniment of the thundering falls close by.

The book "Griswold, a History" mentions Slater's construction...
"In 1846 the old wooden mill was removed and a fine brick mill of greatly increased capacity was erected."

An eight-year-old boy joined me to fish for trout. Here are some of his comments: "caught a four-pound rainbow trout here once... giant carp hide in the dark places. If I caught one it'd pull me in... a muskrat lives under the archway. He's as big as a seal. He likes melon seeds."

apple blossoms

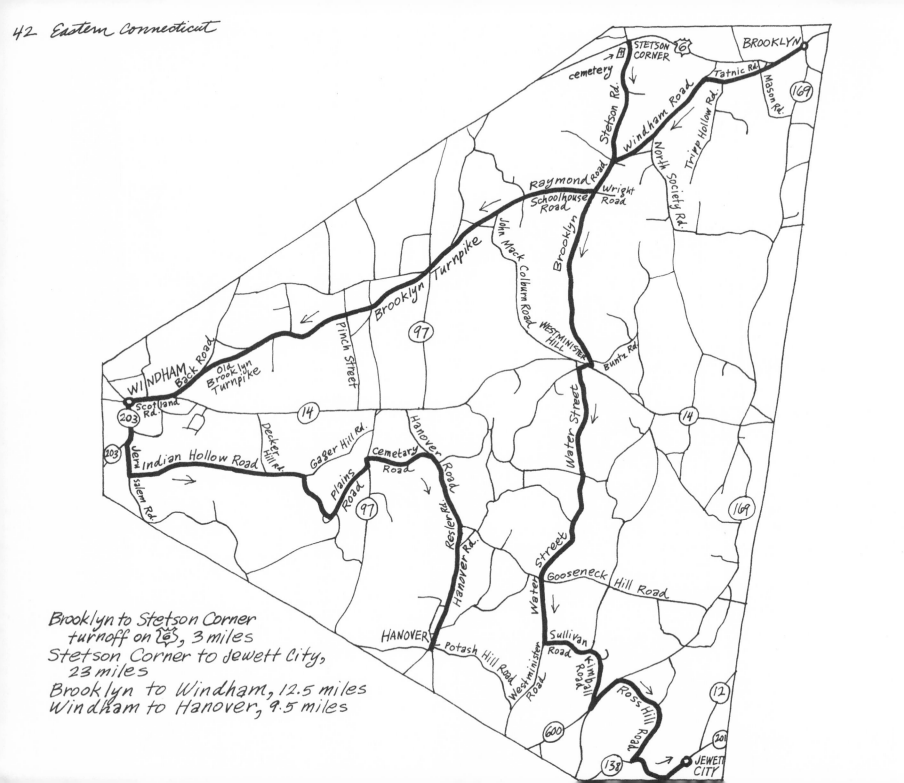

Brooklyn to Stetson Corner
    turnoff on (6), 3 miles
Stetson Corner to Jewett City,
    23 miles
Brooklyn to Windham, 12.5 miles
Windham to Hanover, 9.5 miles

Ruin near Brooklyn

Brooklyn to Windham

At Windham Road and North Society Road is a stone house ruin. I was told that the roof had blown off in the hurricane of 1938. In looking at it today one can study the pioneers' use of stone in the erection of a house wall. This can be done only from the road as the property is privately owned.

I was told by the owner that in the fall, somewhat to his dismay, camera enthusiasts cannot resist clambering on and photographing the ruin nestled as it is amongst the colorful maple tree foliage.

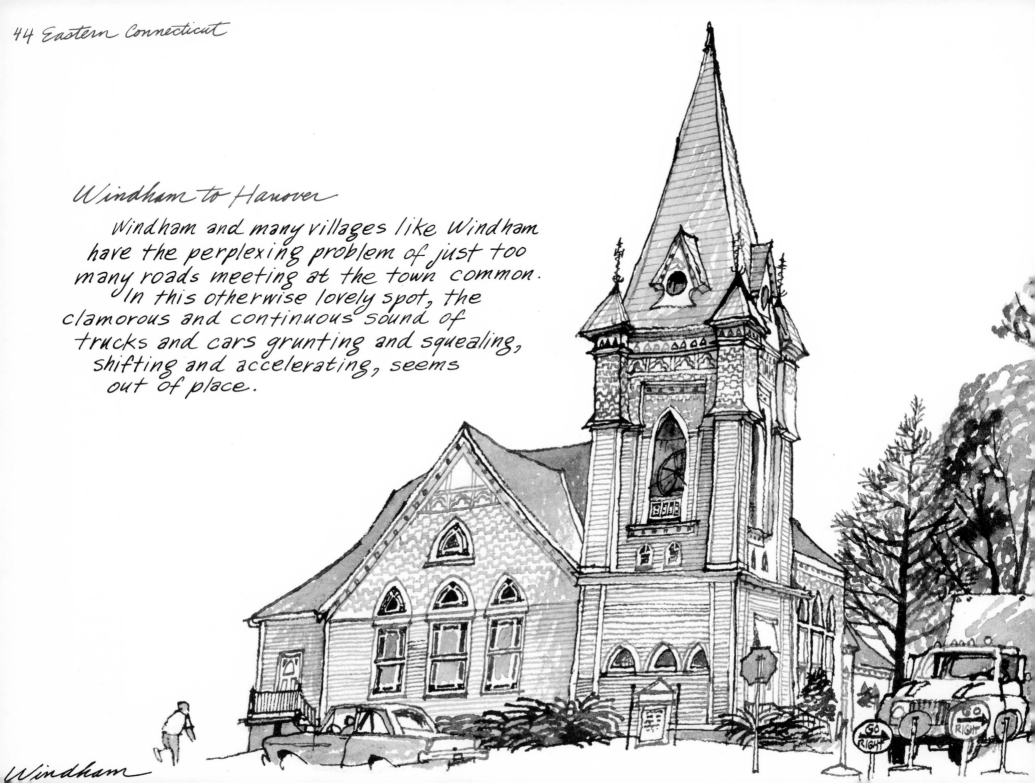

Windham to Hanover

Windham and many villages like Windham have the perplexing problem of just too many roads meeting at the town common. In this otherwise lovely spot, the clamorous and continuous sound of trucks and cars grunting and squealing, shifting and accelerating, seems out of place.

Windham

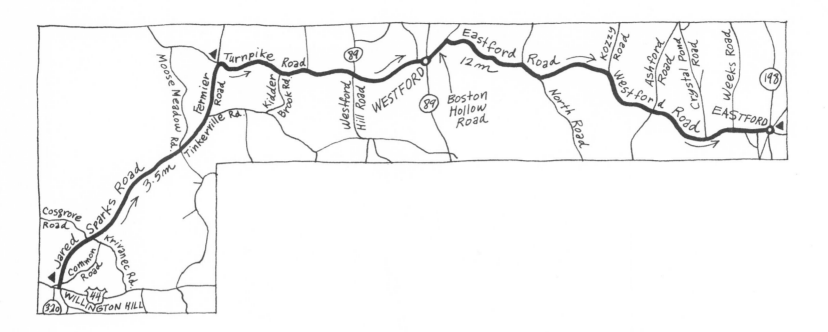

Bluets

Jared Sparks Road, Westford to Eastford

On Boston Hollow Road, Westford, is the Hazen house, also known as the old Barlow Home, now over 200 years old. The addition on the left was once the village store. As I sketched, an unmistakable and most pleasant aroma drifted past my nostrils. Mrs. Hazen was baking apple pies!

The old Barlow home, Westford

NORTH WOODSTOCK

Hagstrom Rd.

Brickyard Road

NORTH GROSVENOR DALE

EAST WOODSTOCK

county Road

Woodstock Road 1.5m

Hibbard Rd.

Fabyan Rd. 4.5m

Red Bridge Rd.

12

Paine District Road

Dugg Hill Road

Ravenville Road

Reardon Road

169

WOODSTOCK

Childs Hill Road

Senexet Road 3.2m

Pulpit Rock Road

Meehan Rd.

Old Hall Rd.

167

SOUTH WOODSTOCK

171

Bassett Hill Rd.

Old Hall Rd.

cutler Hill Rd.

West Quasset Road

East Quasset Road 7.5m

7.5m Quarry Road

198

county Road

EASTFORD Old Colony Road

Sumner Hill Rd.

Swedetown Rd.

Ragged Hill Rd.

no sign

Tyott Road

no sign

Quasset Rd.

97

Mill Bridge Road

East Hill Rd.

622

SHAW HILL

Angel Road

Peterson Rd.

Cassidy Rd.

97

97

Old North Rd.

no sign

97

ABINGTON

44

97

Cheney Road

Covell Road

Babbit Hill Road

.8m

wolf Den Road

Eastford to Woodstock

Eastford to Woodstock is a fine back road sojourn. In Woodstock children whizzed by on bicycles and storm clouds gathered.

church on the common, Woodstock

Three Roads to East Woodstock

My walk in the graveyard was especially rewarding, for beside one memorial grew two mature asparagus. Harvesting them reverently, they proved most tender and sweet at the evening meal.

Road to East Woodstock

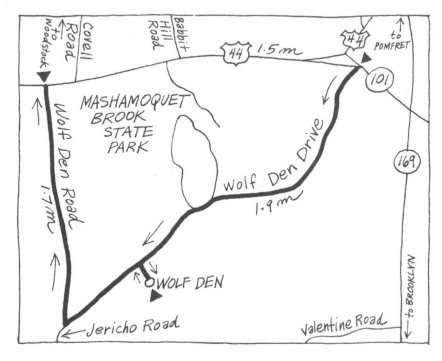

Yellow
Mustard

Wolf Den Road

Along this forest road
in Mashamoquet
Brook State Park you
can park conveniently
and hike to see
the lair of the last
sheep-killing wolf in
Connecticut. Israel
Putnam shot him,
deep in the den,
in 1742.

Israel Putnam Wolf Den, near Pomfret

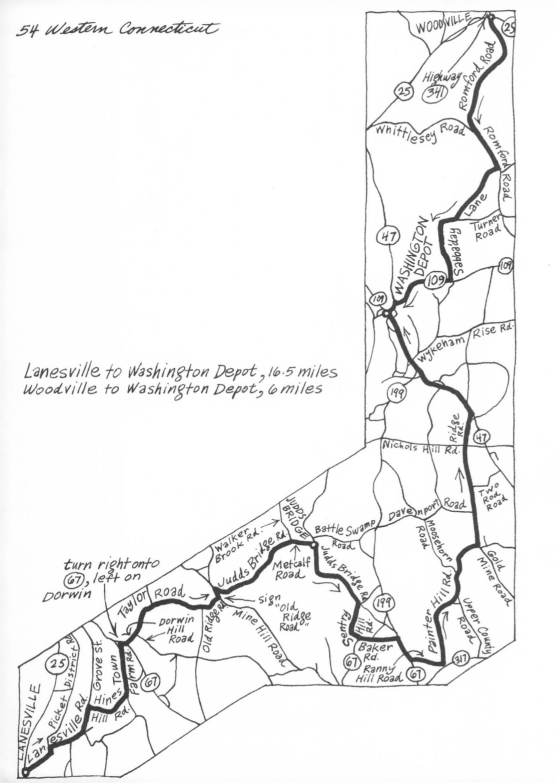

WOODVILLE
25
Highway 341
25
Romford Road
Whittlesey Road
Romford Road
Turner Road
Lane
Sabbaday
47
WASHINGTON DEPOT
109
109
109
Wykeham Rise Rd.
199
Ridge Rd.
47
Nichols Hill Rd.
Two Rod Road
JUDDS BRIDGE
Walker Brook Rd.
Battle Swamp Road
Davenport Road
Judds Bridge Rd.
Moosehorn Road
Gold Mine Road
Metcalf Road
Judds Bridge Rd.
turn right onto 67, left on Dorwin
Judds Bridge Road
199
Painter Hill Rd.
Upper County Road
Taylor Road
Dorwin Hill Road
Old Ridge Rd.
Mine Hill Road
sign "Old Ridge Road"
Sentry Hill Rd.
25
Picket District Rd.
Grove St.
Town Farm Rd.
67
Hines Hill Rd.
Baker Rd.
67
Ranny Hill Road
67
317
LANESVILLE
Lanesville Rd.

Lanesville to Washington Depot, 16.5 miles
Woodville to Washington Depot, 6 miles

Meandering to Washington Depot

Up and down hills, on paved and dirt roads, through the green, green forests of New Milford, Roxbury, and Washington townships one finally emerges at Highway 47 and Washington Depot. As I sketched there, boys canoed expertly down the rushing Shepaug River.

Washington Depot

Roads to Litchfield

Any road to Litchfield, with its many fine colonial mansions, is a pleasure to drive. I couldn't decide which historic house to draw and, as you see, instead sketched this more modest, but colorful old brick building in the shopping area of town.

March Blue Violets

Phelps Block Shops, Litchfield

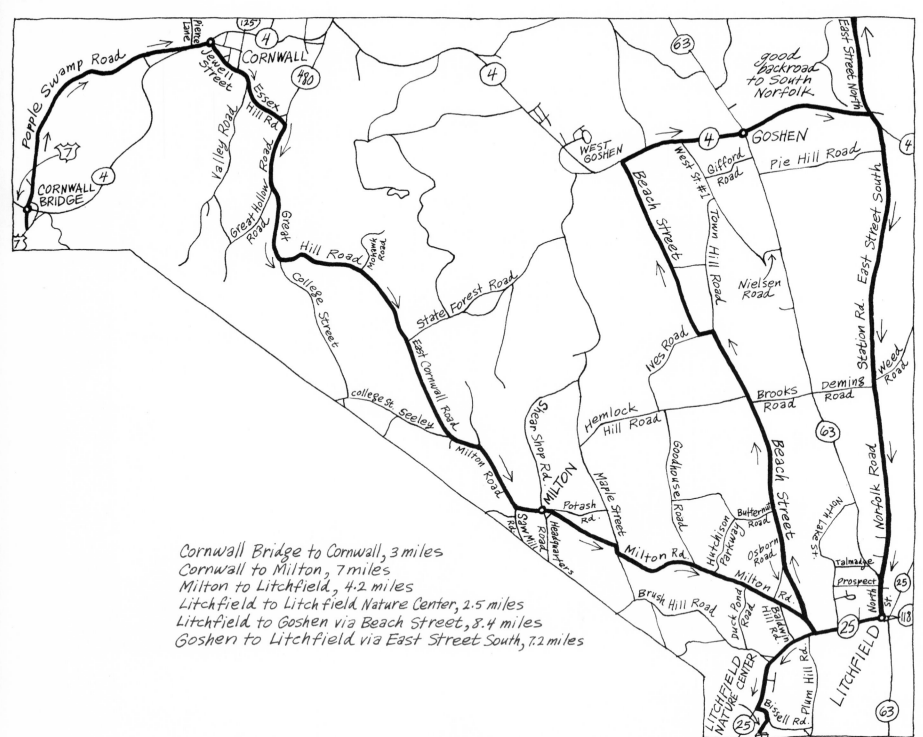

Cornwall Bridge to Cornwall, 3 miles
Cornwall to Milton, 7 miles
Milton to Litchfield, 4.2 miles
Litchfield to Litchfield Nature Center, 2.5 miles
Litchfield to Goshen via Beach Street, 8.4 miles
Goshen to Litchfield via East Street South, 7.2 miles

Southwest of Litchfield

At the White Memorial Foundation's Nature Center were two live screech owls. When I got too close to them one would "clack" his bill and the other make a cricketlike sound. Children were touring through the center as I drew and I received a supreme compliment from one who said, "You draw better than our art teacher!"

Screech Owls, Litchfield Nature Center

Trinity Episcopal Church, 1802, milton

Cornwall Bridge, Cornwall, and Milton to Litchfield

Big, tall white pine grow in the Nature Conservancy sanctuary
along Essex Road. Some seemingly grow from the rock itself.
No one came by as I sketched the old church
in Milton. It seemed a quiet village, indeed.
From here a delightful country road
proceeds to Litchfield.

*White pine and
rock, Essex Hill Road*

Goshen to Litchfield

The big, bright golden eagle distinguishes the Goshen Historical Society building. In the early days this was Eagle Academy, where students could prepare for entrance into Yale University.

Kent Furnace to West Cornwall

The superb Sloane-Stanley Museum of early farm implements begins this back road route through Macedonia Brook State Park to Sharon and West Cornwall.

The big eagle, Goshen Historical Society

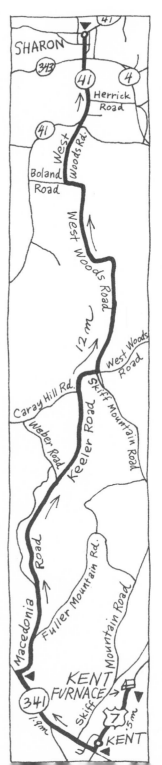

SHARON

343

41

4

Herrick Road

41

West Woods Rd.

Boland Road

West Woods Road

12 m

West Woods Road

Caray Hill Rd.

Weber Road

Skiff Mountain Road

Keeler Road

Fuller Mountain Rd.

Macedonia Road

Mountain Road

KENT FURNACE

341

Skiff

7

.5 m

1.9 m

KENT

PENN. GOOSE-WING
1760

NEW ENGLAND FLARED
Broad axe
1790

N.Y. OVAL BLADE
broad axe
c.1820

BARK SPUDS
c.1760

R.R. TIE BROAD AXE

VERMONT SQUARED
broad axe

SCORING AXE

TRUNNEL MALLET

TRUNNELS (Tree Nails)

"Wheelbarrows were works of art"; Sloane-Stanley Museum, Kent Furnace

The falls, near Falls Village

River Road from West Cornwall

The Housatonic River is right beside you on this road out of West Cornwall. Sometimes trees make a canopy overhead. Just north of Falls Village is an overlook of the great, tumbling falls themselves.

Northern Bush Honeysuckle

WEST Cornwall

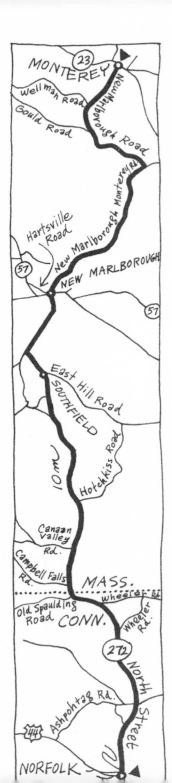

Norfolk to Monterey

The charming town of Norfolk, home of the Yale Summer Music Program, has a splendid Victorian fountain designed by the well-known architect of his time, Stanford White. It serves drinking water to local and itinerant birds, horses, and dogs and I also observed mortals on bicycles drink from the bird dish spout.

Fountain on the common, Norfolk

Massachusetts

Massachusetts has a fascinating network of back roads so extensive that one could fill many books such as this with travel suggestions. My report is mainly concerned with western Massachusetts, an area of great beauty, indeed. I feel that I must congratulate the people of this state and all of New England wherever churches are kept painted, graveyards clipped, historic houses restored, and "progress" resisted whenever it endangered beauty, health, and the preservation of America's historical sites and structures.

Lesser Stitchwort

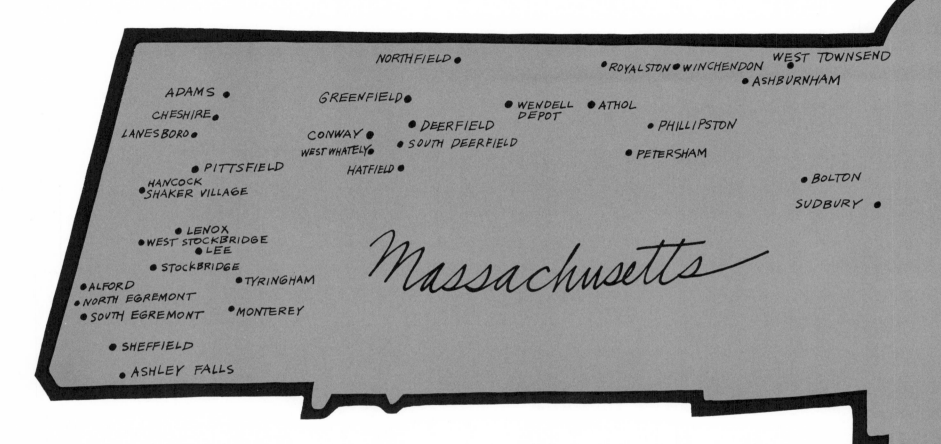

NORTHFIELD •

• ROYALSTON • WINCHENDON   WEST TOWNSEND

• ASHBURNHAM

ADAMS •

GREENFIELD •

• WENDELL   • ATHOL
DEPOT

CHESHIRE •

• DEERFIELD   • PHILLIPSTON

LANESBORO •

CONWAY •

• SOUTH DEERFIELD

WEST WHATELY •

• PETERSHAM

• PITTSFIELD

HATFIELD •

HANCOCK
SHAKER VILLAGE •

• BOLTON

SUDBURY •

• LENOX
• WEST STOCKBRIDGE
• LEE

• STOCKBRIDGE

Massachusetts

• ALFORD   • TYRINGHAM
• NORTH EGREMONT
• SOUTH EGREMONT   • MONTEREY

• SHEFFIELD

• ASHLEY FALLS

Road to Tyringham

Tyringham is a lovely, green valley enclosed on three sides by mountains. Mark Twain knew this area in his time and in the summer artists, writers, and musicians still come to live in the valley.

From 1792 to 1894 Tyringham was the site of a large Shaker settlement, and many of their homes hereabouts are still in use.

Tyringham Galleries occupy the "Gingerbread House," built in the 30s to the bizarre taste of sculptor, Henry Kitson.

"Gingerbread House", Tyringham

From 44, Weotogue Road to
Bartholemew's Cobble, 3.7 miles
Ashley Falls to 7 at Brookside
Road, 10 miles

Gill-over-
the-ground

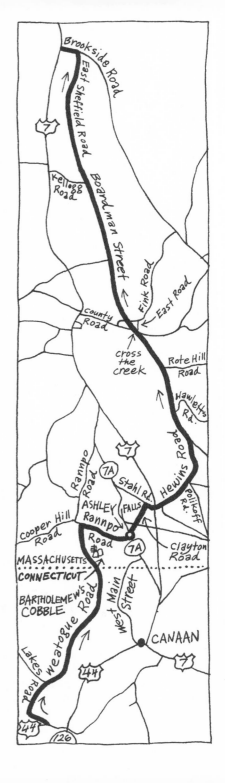

Bartholomew's Cobble

Weotogue Road and Bartholomew's Cobble

Weotogue Road and its farms and pastures, meadows and river views passes Bartholomew's Cobble, an area preserved for man in all its infinite beauty. The late Mark Van Doren wrote of the Cobble in 1970, "a little marble mountain upon whose sides grow trees of ancient origin and plants of unimaginable age. May nothing ever threaten its serenity."

Sheffield to South Egremont to Stockbridge

This is a wonderful collection of farm and forest back roads. In Alford, along the way, stop to walk among the tall graveyard monuments. There was a bit of competition, I imagine, as to whose stone memorial would be highest.

Egremont Town Hall, 1822

Included in this drawing of Stockbridge's colorful main street is Norman Rockwell's old studio, with its second-story picture window.

WILLIAMS & SONS

Stockbridge market

COUNTRY STORE

BARBER SHOP

Stockbridge

78

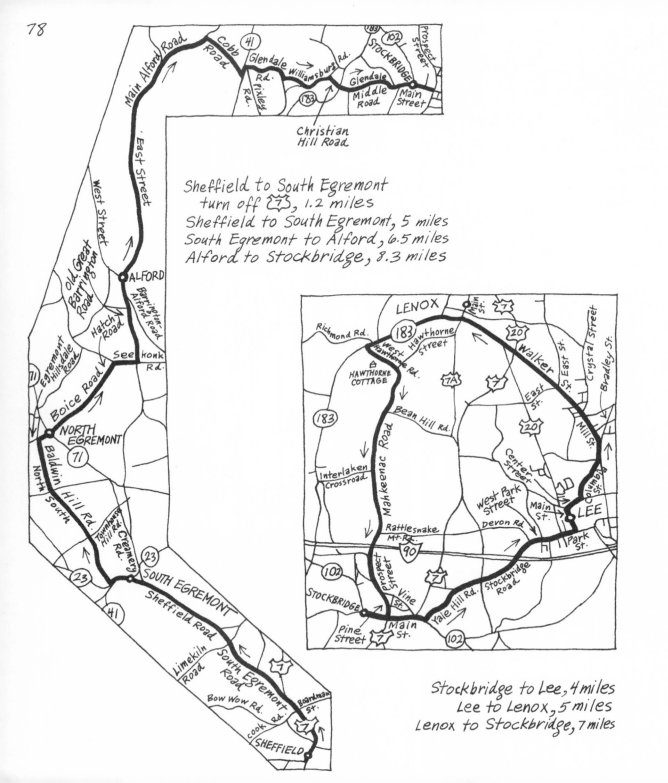

Sheffield to South Egremont
turn off 7, 1.2 miles
Sheffield to South Egremont, 5 miles
South Egremont to Alford, 6.5 miles
Alford to Stockbridge, 8.3 miles

Stockbridge to Lee, 4 miles
Lee to Lenox, 5 miles
Lenox to Stockbridge, 7 miles

Edgewood
Farm near Lee

Stockbridge Loop

Along Yale Hill Road one dewy morning I sketched this barn. The road leads directly into the paper-mill town of Lee, with its big white church on the common. I traveled Walker Street to Lenox and then back past Lake Mahkeenac to Stockbridge.

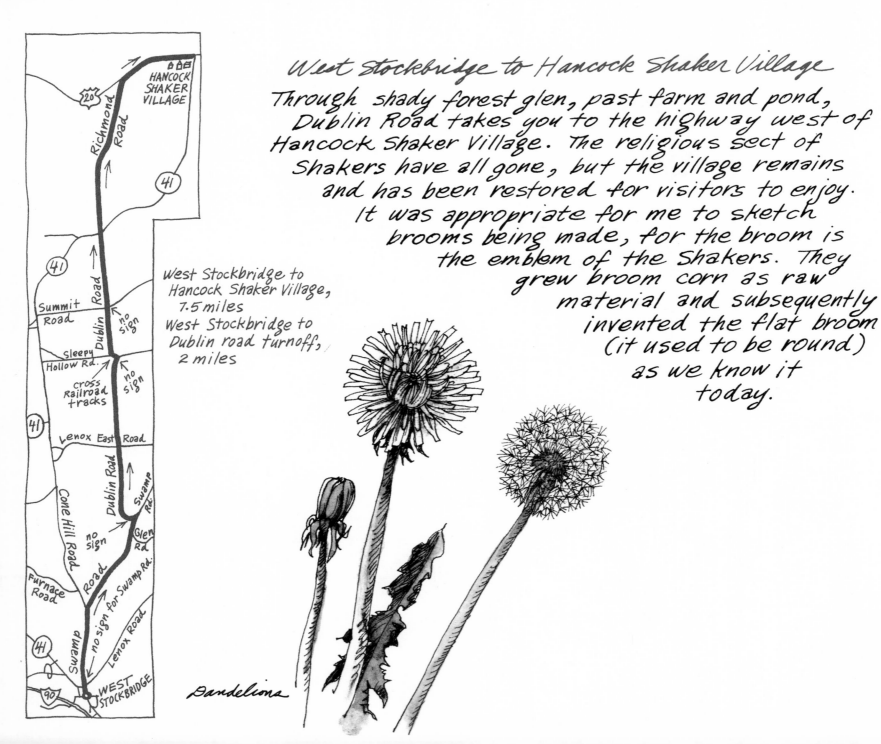

West Stockbridge to Hancock Shaker Village, 7.5 miles
West Stockbridge to Dublin road turnoff, 2 miles

West Stockbridge to Hancock Shaker Village

Through shady forest glen, past farm and pond, Dublin Road takes you to the highway west of Hancock Shaker Village. The religious sect of Shakers have all gone, but the village remains and has been restored for visitors to enjoy. It was appropriate for me to sketch brooms being made, for the broom is the emblem of the Shakers. They grew broom corn as raw material and subsequently invented the flat broom (it used to be round) as we know it today.

Dandelions

Broom vises, Hancock Shaker Village

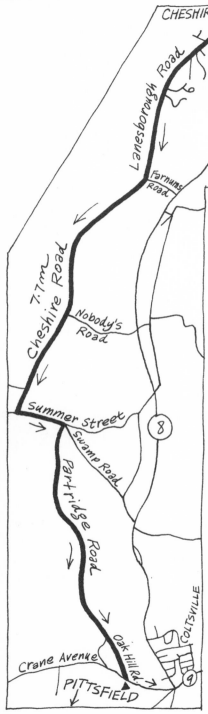

CHESHIRE

Lanesborough Road

Farnums Road

7.7m

Cheshire Road

Nobody's Road

Summer Street

8

Swamp Road

Partridge Road

COLTSVILLE

Crane Avenue

Oak Hill Rd.

PITTSFIELD

9

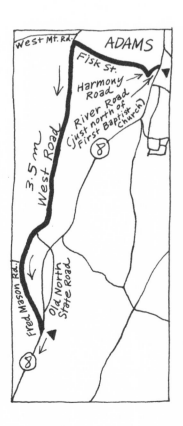

West Mt. Rd.

ADAMS

Fisk St.

Harmony Road

River Road (just north of First Baptist Church)

3.5m

West Road

8

Fred Mason Rd.

Old North State Road

8

Adams to Pittsfield

From Adams off Highway 8 there is a country road south that begins at River Road, just north of the First Baptist Church. Where the road returns to Route 8 again you can travel on it south and exit at Lanesboro Road, which will again permit a tranquil pace to Pittsfield.

Farm on Fred Mason Road, Cheshire

Williamsburg to Conway

Forest scenery, babbling brooks, and a good
   dirt road from West Whately bring you down
the hill to Conway. Approaching
   a village such as this on a
country road, I've found, helps

*Covered Bridge,
Conway*

church
116
to Deerfield →
116
CONWAY
covered bridge
Hill View Rd.
Academy Road
Dump Rd.
West Whately Rd.
Cricket Hill Rd.
5.5 m.
Roaring Brook Road
Conway Rd.
Dog Hill Road
WEST WHATELY
4.5 m.
Nash Hill Rd.
Oneill Road
Depot Rd.
→ to Williamsburg
9
↘ to Northampton

give one an even greater sense
of the history of the town.
  I was brought out of my horse
  and buggy reverie somewhat
as occasional autos and trucks
using the covered bridge I was
  sketching passed and layered
me with dust. I mused that
horses and buggies would have
done the same.

Conway to Deerfield

  In the most beautiful
village of Deerfield, from
1732 to 1780, Reverend
Jonathan Ashley, preacher
and "Tory", resided behind
this unpainted, marvelously
weathered door.

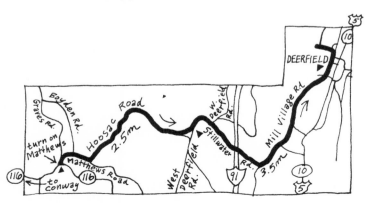

Ashley House
entrance,
Deerfield

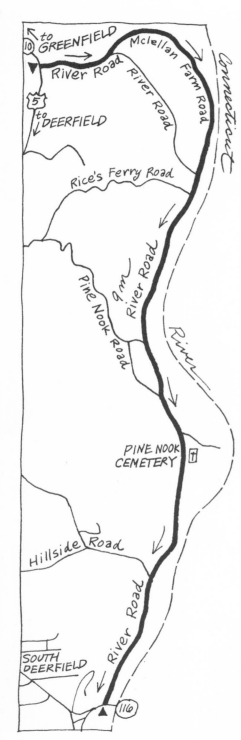

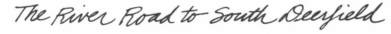
The River Road to South Deerfield

The Connecticut River is close
  by and farms and fields fill
the landscape. I sketched at Pine Nook
  cemetery on the banks of the Connecticut
listening to bird calls at the time of
    the setting sun.

Pine Nook Cemetery
River Road to South Deerfield

PINE NOOK CEMETERY

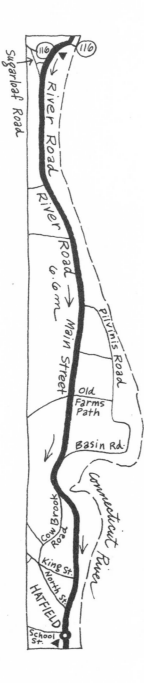

Sugarloaf Road

116 116

River Road

River Road

River Road 6.6 m →

Main Street

Pilivinis Road

Old Farms Path

Basin Rd.

Connecticut River

Cow Brook

King St.

North St.

HATFIELD

School St.

River Road to Hatfield

Along this road are vast fields of tobacco and their attendant long curing barns.

I sketched a more classic barn belonging to John Olynik. He had come from the Ukraine in 1913 and told me as I drew, "I know that barn 60 year. They want me to take top off barn. I no let them." In 1917 flood waters were four feet high in the barn. It stood firm, as it does today, made for the ages with its heavy timbers fastened together in old-fashioned mortise and tenon construction.

Robin Plantain

John Olynik barn, River Road near Hatfield

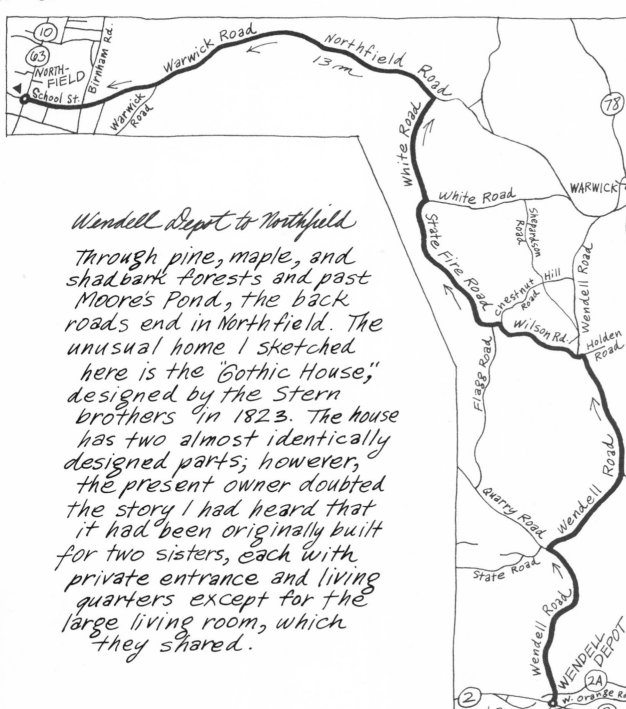

Wendell Depot to Northfield

Through pine, maple, and shadbark forests and past Moore's Pond, the back roads end in Northfield. The unusual home I sketched here is the "Gothic House," designed by the Stern brothers in 1823. The house has two almost identically designed parts; however, the present owner doubted the story I had heard that it had been originally built for two sisters, each with private entrance and living quarters except for the large living room, which they shared.

Gothic House, Northfield

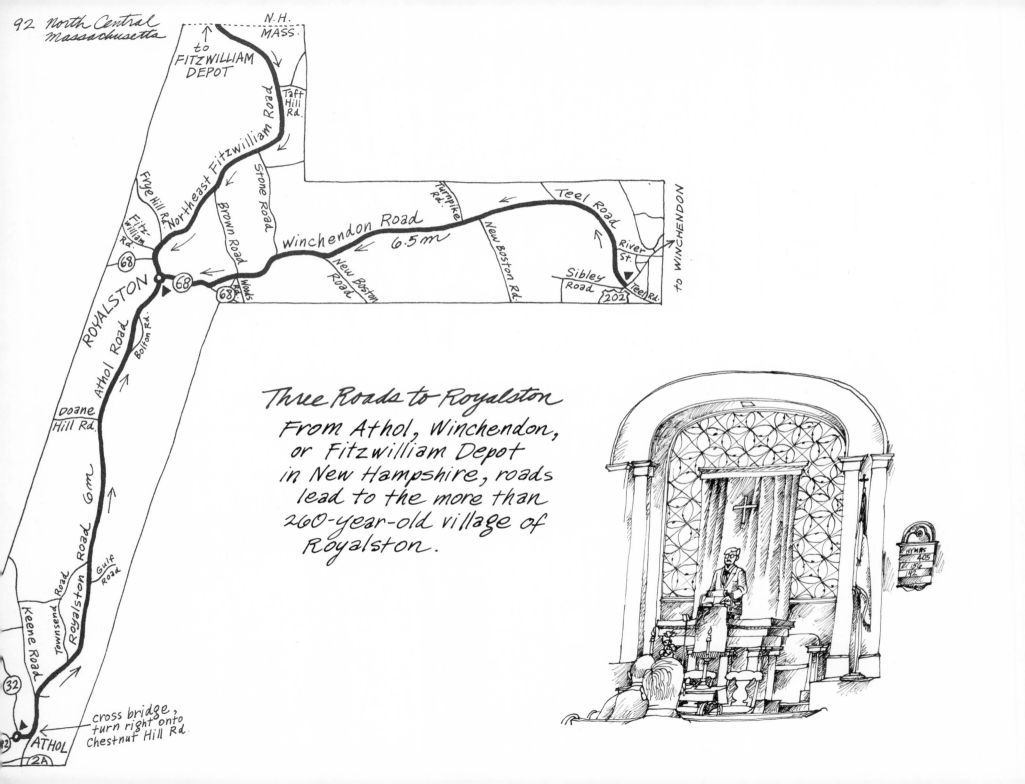

N.H.
MASS.

to FITZWILLIAM DEPOT

Taft Hill Rd.

Northeast Fitzwilliam Road

Frye Hill Rd.

Stone Road

Brown Road

Fitz-william Rd.

68

ROYALSTON

68

68

Woods Rd.

Turnpike Rd.

Winchendon Road 6.5 m

New Boston Road

New Boston Rd.

Teel Road

River St.

to WINCHENDON

Sibley Road

Teel Rd.

202

Athol Road

Bolton Rd.

Doane Hill Rd.

Royalston Road 6 m

Gulf Road

Townsend Road

Keene Road

32

32

2A

ATHOL

cross bridge, turn right onto Chestnut Hill Rd.

Three Roads to Royalston

From Athol, Winchendon, or Fitzwilliam Depot in New Hampshire, roads lead to the more than 260-year-old village of Royalston.

HYMNS
405
156
142

It was Sunday and I not only sketched the exterior of the handsome Congregational church but also attended the service! A parishioner told me during coffee time later that there is a nest of hornets somewhere back of the chandelier and on hot, summer Sundays, these hornets in their torpor, have been known to drop on worshippers during service.

Congregational Church, 1820
Royalston

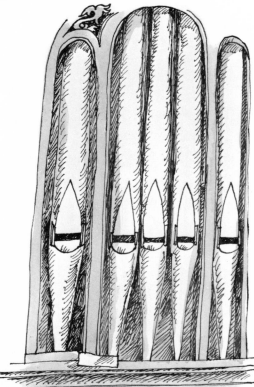

Petersham to Philipston

Petersham country store has been
serving the community since 1840.
Only for a short period of time
was it a hat factory.
The village of Petersham, directly
south of Athol, was settled
in 1733 and named after Petersham
in Surrey, England.

Royalston.
Congregational church organ
made by William A. Johnson, 1863

Germond's
Country Store,
Petersham

marsh Marigold

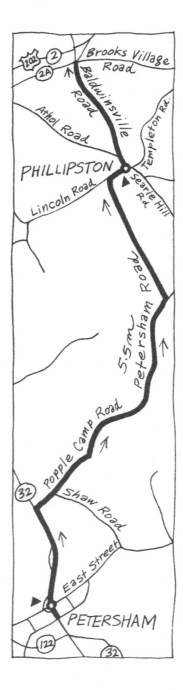

Philipston's 1785 church has a faceless, century-old, wooden-geared clock in its tower. To preserve the precious wooden parts an electric striker now hits the 1840 bell in the belfry.

Without asking permission, village boys
chimed the bell in my honor,
pulling heartily on the belfry rope,
then posed in front of the church
for me to sketch. I looked
around for concerned,
advancing adults, but
none came.

church of the faceless clock,
Phillipston

The Way to Ashburnham

1975 marks the 100th birthday for Eclipse #2 Firehouse. A country road drive to Ashburnham starts here at New Fitchburg Road. Where South Road comes in there is a marker telling how, in the early days, Fitch (for whom the town of Fitchburg is named) and his family were kidnapped by Indians, taken to Canada and held for ransom.

ECLIPSE CO. NO. 2 T.F.D

Eclipse Fire Engine Company No. 2, North Townsend

WEST TOWNSEND

West Townsend to Ashburnham, 11 miles

119

Old Battery Road

New Fitchburg Rd.

Lunenberg Rd.

Vinton Pond Rd.

Townsend Street

New W. Townsend Road 3.5m

Howard Street

Wares Road

31

Stewart Road

Old Northfield Road

Richardson Road

31

South Road

Richardson Road 5m

Rindge Road

Turnpike

Piper Rd.

Wilker Rd.

LANE HOUSE

Jewell Hill Rd.

Crosby Rd.

Russell Hill Road

Ashburnham Street
(also called "Russell Hill Rd.")

101

ASHBURNHAM

Kelton Rd.

Styx River Rd.

12

Wild Geranium

Yellow Rattle

Lane House, 1810, Russell Hill Road, Ashburnham

Flowering Dogwood

Sudbury to Bolton

Along this way is Mrs. Meigs' house, originally colonial in design with later additions of a victorian style. The house is on Randall Street near the golf course and golf balls occasionally pepper the 18th-century house. Mrs. Meigs said that her cat, a skunk, and a large woodchuck spent the winter under the porch.

The woodchuck even made an appearance for me while I was there.

Sudbury to Bolton, 12.3 miles

Mrs. Meig's "Saltbox Victorian"

On Old Sandwich Road

I sketched Plymouth town from the yacht club
and continued south toward Cape Cod on
Old Sandwich Road, past lovely estates,
and through sometimes dense
pitch pine forests.

Plymouth

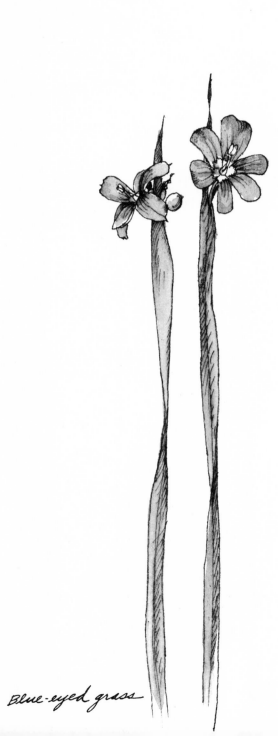

Blue-eyed grass

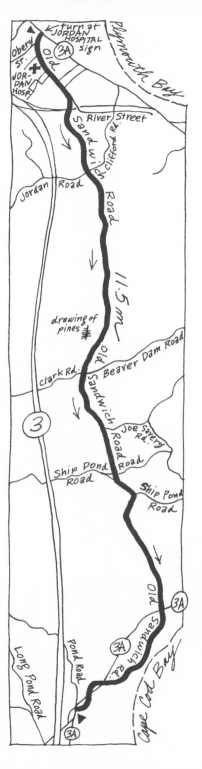

Beach plum blossoms

Old Sandwich Road

Provincetown

The Old Road to Provincetown

The old road is Cranberry Highway (Highway 6A), bypassed today by the fast U.S. Highway 6. This is the only "back road" in this book that is busy and highly populated; however, the Cape towns along each coast are of infinite interest and I wish to suggest their exploration.

Old Highway 28 and 28A and County Road can be the basis for exploring the ocean coast on the return trip.

Vermont

Vermont is the state for back roads.
They are mostly dirt but well graded.
In Connecticut, Massachusetts, and
Rhode Island vistas are obscured by trees,
but Vermont rewards one's eyes with open,
rolling farm landscape and also
picturesque views of approaching
towns. And the land seems more
remote here from urban
influences.

Birdfoot Trefoil

110

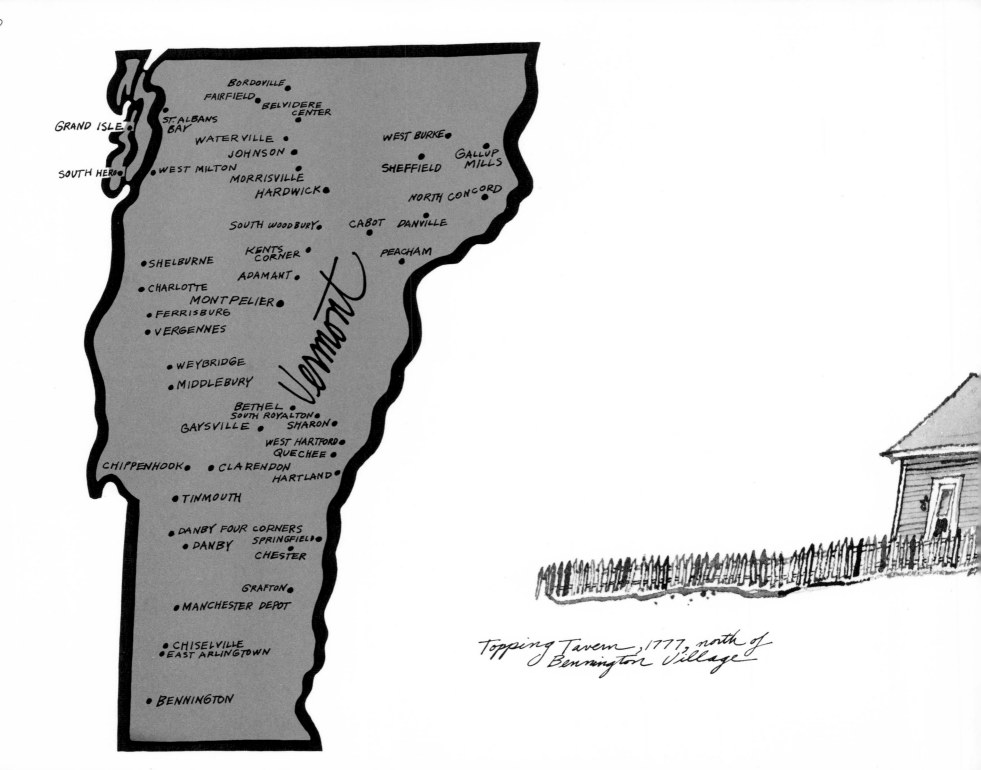

Topping Tavern, 1777, north of
Bennington Village

Bennington to East Arlington

Lady Gosford, who liked to be called Beatrice, countess of Gosford, bought this old tavern in 1926, and through her devotion and care it stands today along the old stagecoach road to East Arlington. When she first saw the tavern she said, "It's simply topping!" And that's how it got its present name, so I've been told.

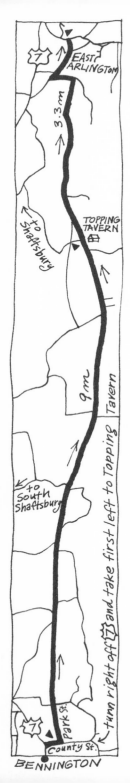

EAST ARLINGTON

7

3.3 m

to Shaftsbury

TOPPING TAVERN

9 m

to South Shaftsburg

turn right off 7 and take first left to Topping Tavern

7

Park St.

County St.

BENNINGTON

MANCHESTER

7

SUNDERLAND

7

SUNDERLAND STATION

8 m

to Arlington

covered bridge
CHISELVILLE

KANSAS

Rd. from Topping Tavern

EAST ARLINGTON

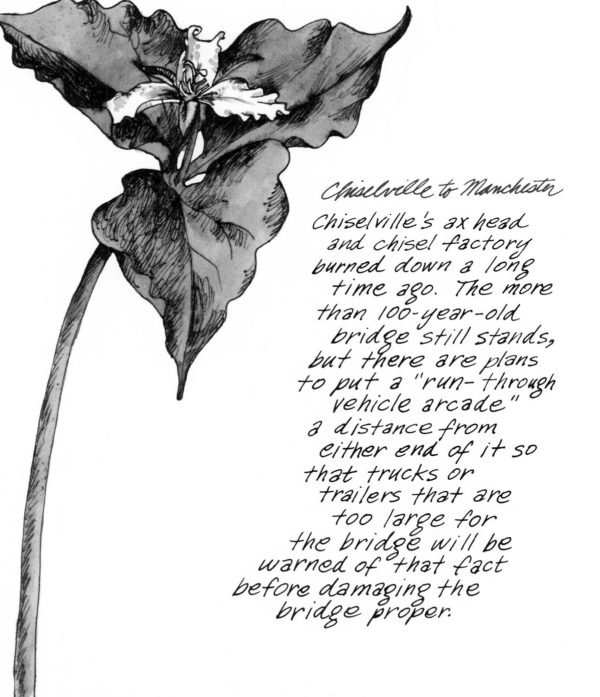

Chiselville to Manchester

Chiselville's ax head and chisel factory burned down a long time ago. The more than 100-year-old bridge still stands, but there are plans to put a "run-through vehicle arcade" a distance from either end of it so that trucks or trailers that are too large for the bridge will be warned of that fact before damaging the bridge proper.

Painted Trillium

ONE DOLLAR FINE
FOR DRIVING FASTER THAN A
WALK ON THIS BRIDGE.

Chiselville Bridge

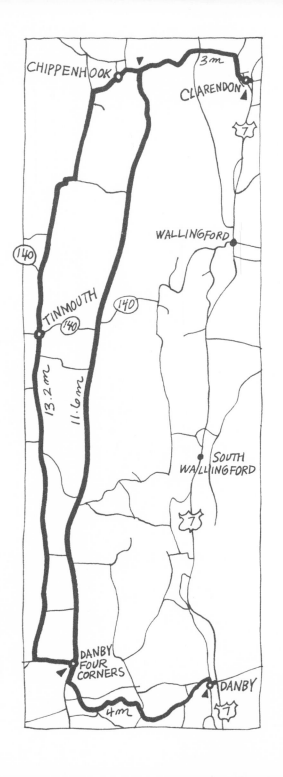

Jack
in the Pulpit

*Danby to Chippenhook
and Clarendon*

Pearl Buck lived in Danby the
last years of her life and
walked through the village each
day, recognizable immediately
by the oriental robe she
wore. The village bookshop
was well known to her and
today sells Pearl Buck books
almost exclusively.

Up the hill from Danby
two parallel back roads
go north from Danby Four
Corners past farm, forest, and
mountain scenery toward
Tinmouth and Chippenhook.

The Village Bookshop, Danby

To South Royalton and Bethel

A very interesting and meandering road along the White River takes you to South Royalton and Bethel. The horseshoe-shaped "Handy Memorial" on South Royalton's common is engraved, "In honor of Hannah Hunter Handy who rescued 9 children from the Indians at the burning of Royalton, Oct. 16, 1780, after she married Gideon Mosher of Sharon, Vt."

Also engraved are the words, "Phineas Parkhurst who was shot at the Indian raid rode with a bullet in his side to Lebanon, New Hampshire, giving the alarm.

On the green,
South Royalton

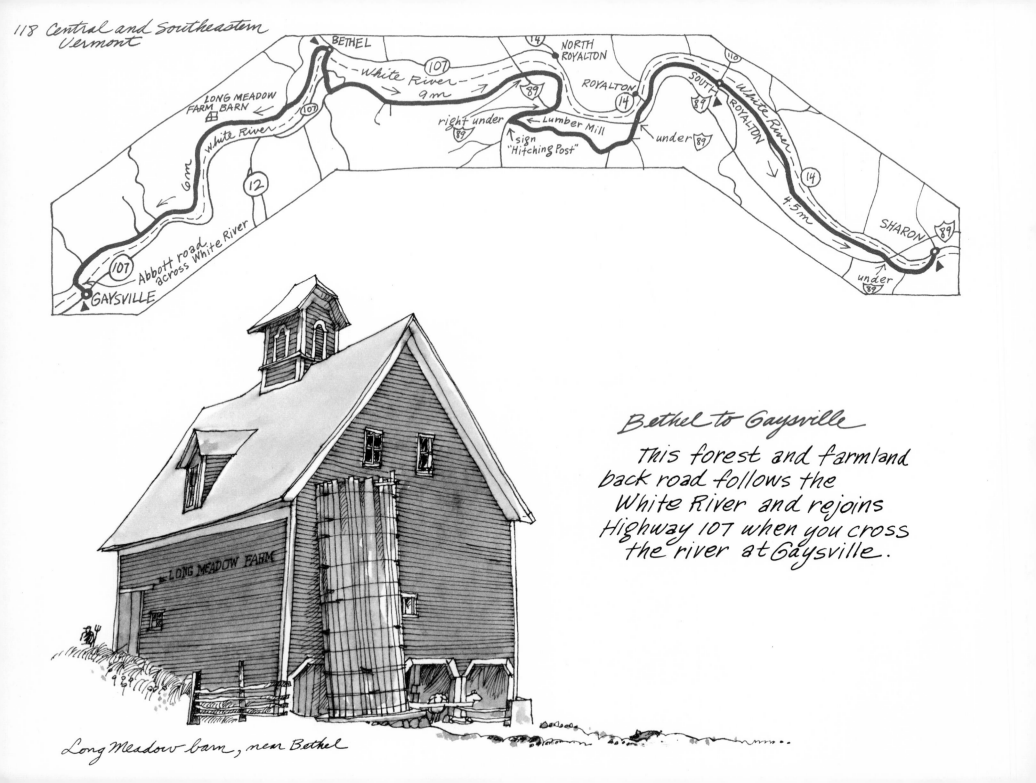

BETHEL

LONG MEADOW FARM BARN

White River 9m

107

6m White River

12

Abbott road across White River

107

GAYSVILLE

14

NORTH ROYALTON

89

ROYALTON

14

right under 89

Lumber Mill

sign "Hitching Post"

under 89

110

SOUTH ROYALTON

89

White River

14

4.5m

SHARON

89

under 89

Bethel to Gaysville

This forest and farmland back road follows the White River and rejoins Highway 107 when you cross the river at Gaysville.

LONG MEADOW FARM

Long Meadow barn, near Bethel

Millpond at Quechee

120

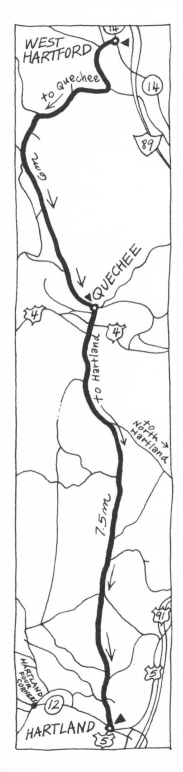

Lily of the Valley

Road to Quechee

The dam upriver
was holding the
Ottauquechee River
back on the day I was
in Quechee. It would
be more dramatic to
see the water crashing
down the whole expanse
of river, I would imagine.
I sketched from
Quechee's new covered
bridge, then drove the
forest road to Hartland.

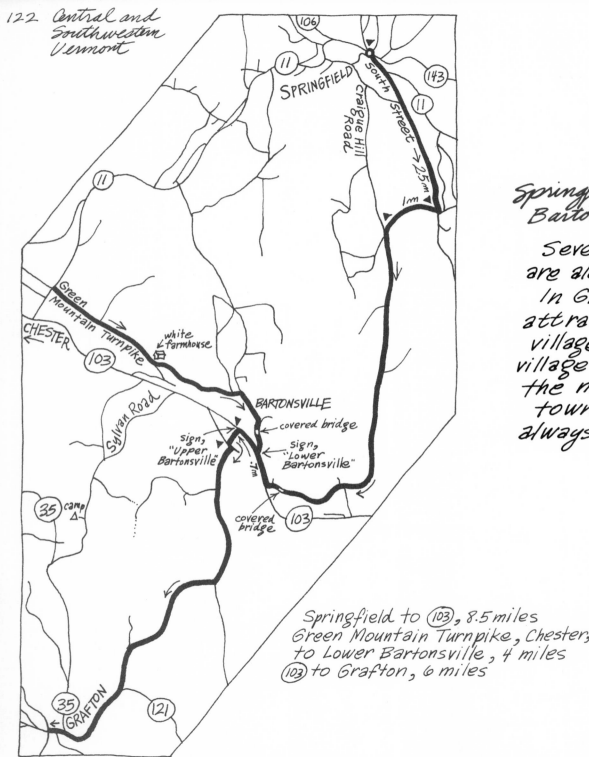

106

11

SPRINGFIELD

143

11

South Street → 2.5m

Craigue Hill Road

1m

11

Green Mountain Turnpike

CHESTER

103

white farmhouse

Sylvan Road

BARTONSVILLE

← covered bridge

sign, "Upper Bartonsville"

sign, "Lower Bartonsville"

.7m

35

camp △

covered bridge

103

35

GRAFTON

121

Springfield or Chester to Bartonsville and Grafton

Several covered bridges are along these roads.

In Grafton, a tidy and attractive Vermont village, I sketched the village store and observed the nice people of the town coming and going, always a pleasant pastime.

Springfield to (103), 8.5 miles
Green Mountain Turnpike, Chester, to Lower Bartonsville, 4 miles
(103) to Grafton, 6 miles

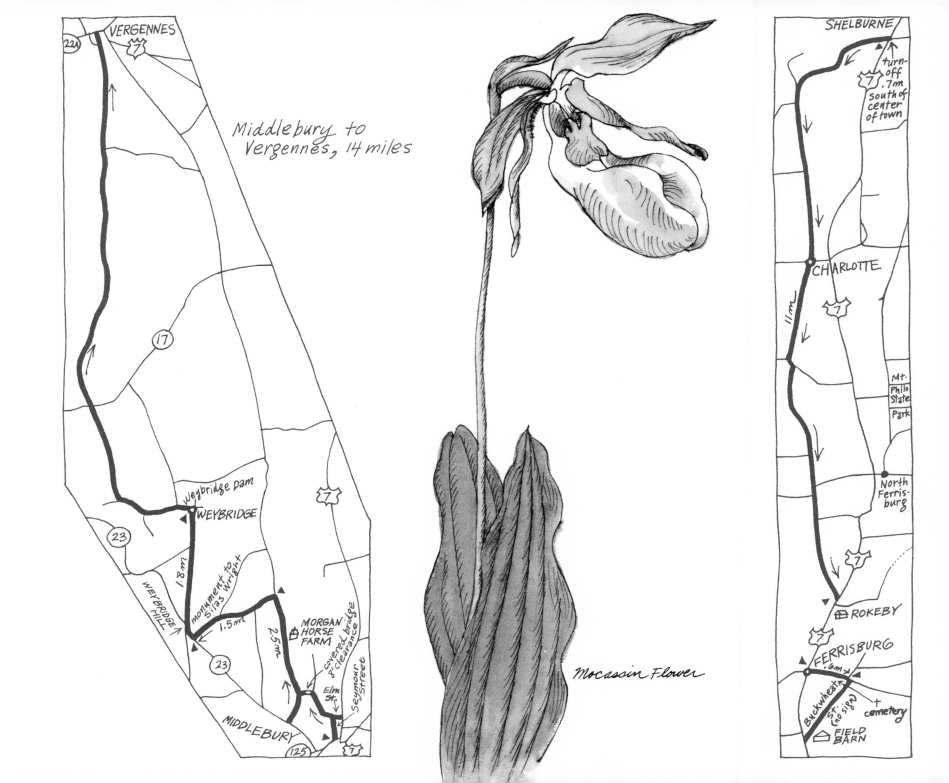

Left map:

22A

VERGENNES

7

Middlebury to
Vergennes, 14 miles

17

Weybridge Dam
WEYBRIDGE

23

1.8m

Weybridge Hill

monument to
Silas Wright

1.5m

2.5m

MORGAN
HORSE
FARM

covered bridge
8' clearance

23

Elm
St.

Seymour Street

7

MIDDLEBURY

125

7

Center illustration:

Mocassin Flower

Right map:

SHELBURNE

turn-off
.7m
south of
center
of town

7

CHARLOTTE

7

1.1m

Mt.
Philo
State
Park

7

North
Ferris-
burg

7

ROKEBY

7

FERRISBURG

.6m

Buckwheat
St. (no sign)

cemetery

FIELD
BARN

Middlebury to Vergennes

For great distances you can see eye-pleasing views of gently rolling hills, prosperous looking farms and farmland. South of the village of Weybridge is the Morgan Horse Farm where America's first breed of horse, the Morgan, is bred and raised by the University of Vermont.

The horse, Justin Morgan, was born in 1789, and so distinctive was he, sired by an English thorougbred and a mare of Arabian extraction it is believed, that his line has been carefully bred to this day.

Morgan Horse Farm, Weybridge

Rokeby, Ferrisburg

Rokeby to Charlotte
and Shelburne

North of Fernisburg is
Rokeby, the ancestral
home of Rowland E.
Robinson, Vermont's
19th-century artist,
illustrator, writer and
folklorist. His home, still
completely furnished with
the Robinson furniture
and effects, is open to
visitors during the summer
months. Rowland's daughter,
Rachael, had sketched her
father in the 1890s, so using her
original drawing I recreated him
for you, sitting beside his
kitchen fireplace almost 90
years ago.

Ferrisburg to Buckwheat Street

The Robinson family is buried at the cemetery near Buckwheat Street. Karl Field's eleven-sided barn designed in 1911 is also located on this old country road, once a main road.

Polygonal barn, Ferrisburg

Lake Champlain Back Road

Boat rigs like this one are a necessity for raising and lowering boats into the lake. They are on wheels and can be pulled ashore before winter's freeze.

Along this back road, at Miltonboro's shady cemetery, graves hold the remains of people who lived in the 1700s.

Boat rig, Lake Champlain

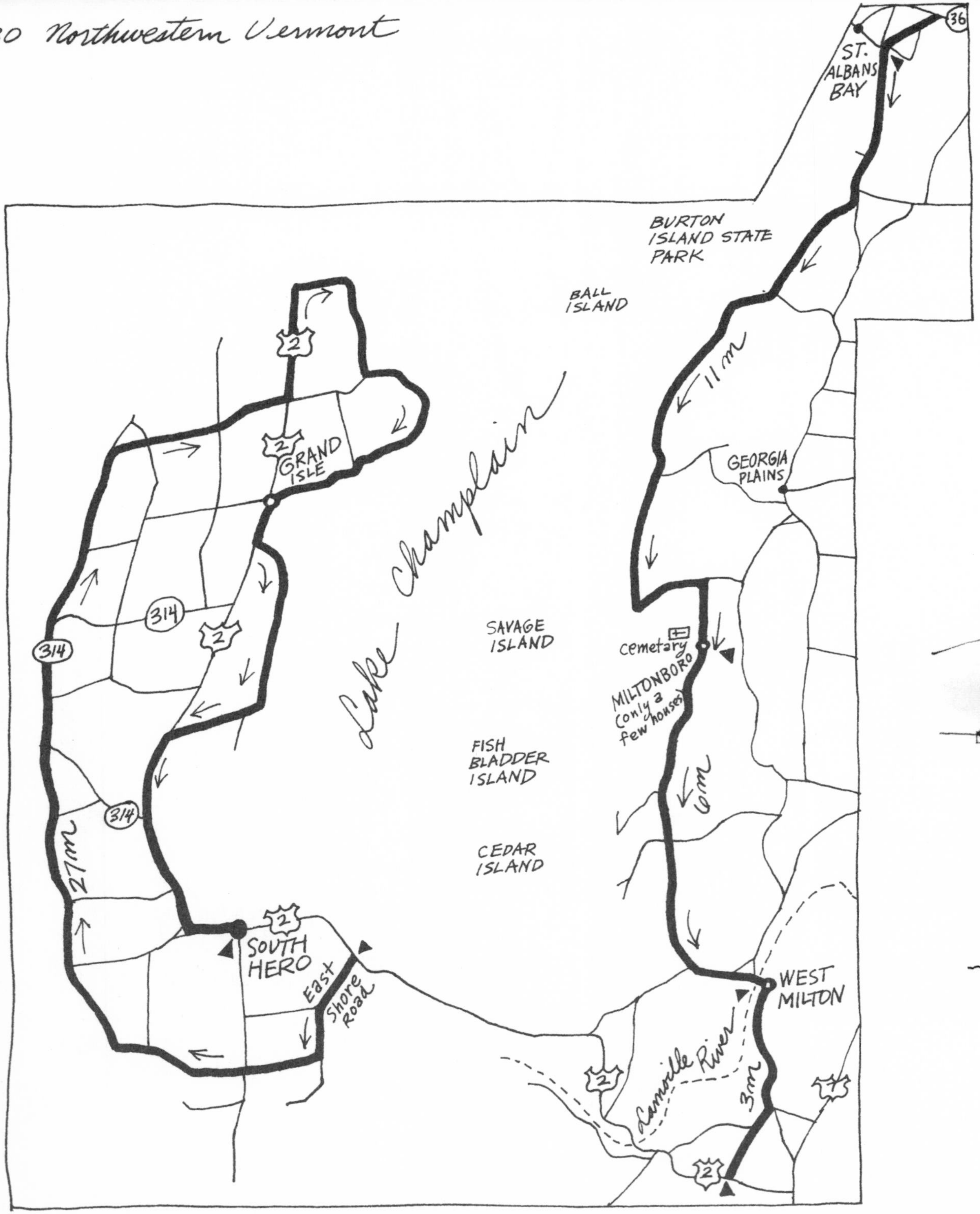

ST. ALBANS BAY

36

BURTON ISLAND STATE PARK

BALL ISLAND

11 m

GEORGIA PLAINS

2

GRAND ISLE

314

2

Lake Champlain

SAVAGE ISLAND

cemetary

MILTONBORO (only a few houses)

FISH BLADDER ISLAND

314

27 m

CEDAR ISLAND

2

SOUTH HERO

East Shore Road

West Milton

Lamoille River

2

3 m

7

2

Grand Isle, Lake Champlain

Grand Isle and South Hero

Back roads pass through rolling countryside, farmed
 by Americans since the Revolution when war heroes
received land grants. In 1783 this area joined the
"Free and Independent Republic of Vermont."

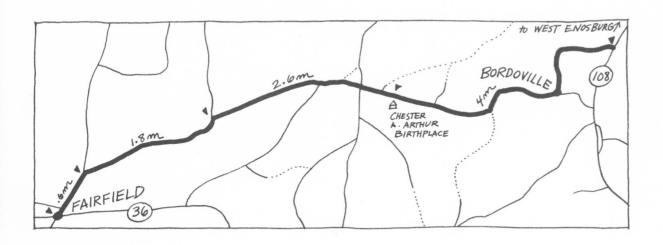

Fairfield to Bordoville

There are long views of attractive farming
land along this country road. Near Bordoville
is the birthplace of our 21st United States
president, Chester A. Arthur.

On the road, Fairfield to Bordoville

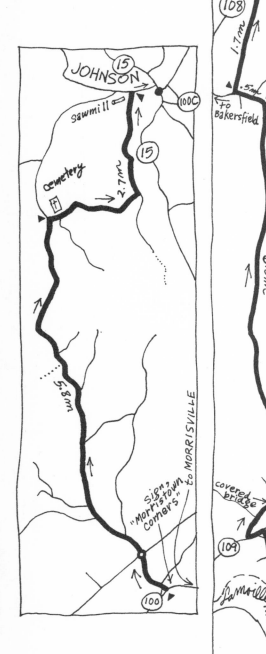

108

108

1.7m

.5m

←to Bakersfield

6.5m

109

covered brige

3m

BELVIDERE CENTER

covered brige

109

BELVIDERE JUNCTION

3.5m

←covered bridge

←covered brige

109

covered bridge→

WATERVILLE

109

Lamoille River

5.5m

1.7 miles from JOHNSON

15

15

15

JOHNSON

sawmill

15

Cemetery

2.7m

5.8m

Sign, "Morristown Corners"

to MORRISVILLE

100

100C

Morrisville to Johnson

Arriving at Johnson from Morrisville is unique in that the road passes through a working lumber mill. I got permission to sketch the "log de-barker" and emerged from the experience with ears ringing and bark chips down my neck. The logs on the right are having their bark removed by the churning saw blade. Those on the left are on their way to be sawed into planks.

Log de-barker, Manchester Lumber Company,
Johnson

Johnson to Waterville

It is a pleasant drive from Johnson to Waterville along the meandering Lamoille River.

The bandstand in Waterville used to bulge with 22 musicians on concert nights, but that was decades ago. The Town Hall was once a church, then a library. The clock tower was added to get sufficient height for its pendulum.

WATERVILLE
SETTLED BY
TIMOTHY BROWN
AND WIFE
MEREDITH WARD BROWN
1779

Town Hall, Waterville

SOUTH
WOODBURY

3.6 m

14

Nelson
Pond

Mirror
Lake

NORTH
CALAIS

2.8 m

MAPLE
CORNER

1837
Tavern

KENTS
CORNER

2 m

1.5 m

ADAMANT

To Kents Corner and
South Woodbury

Mirror Lake is passed on
this route and Nelson Pond
is circled. Only one
fisherman's boat broke
the surface of this placid
body of water on that
day in June.

6 m

EAST
MONTPELIER
CENTER

12

MONTPELIER
STATE
CAPITOL

2

Main
St.

.6 m

Take Main
Street north
from
Montpelier

Spring
St.

12

Nelson Pond, Calais

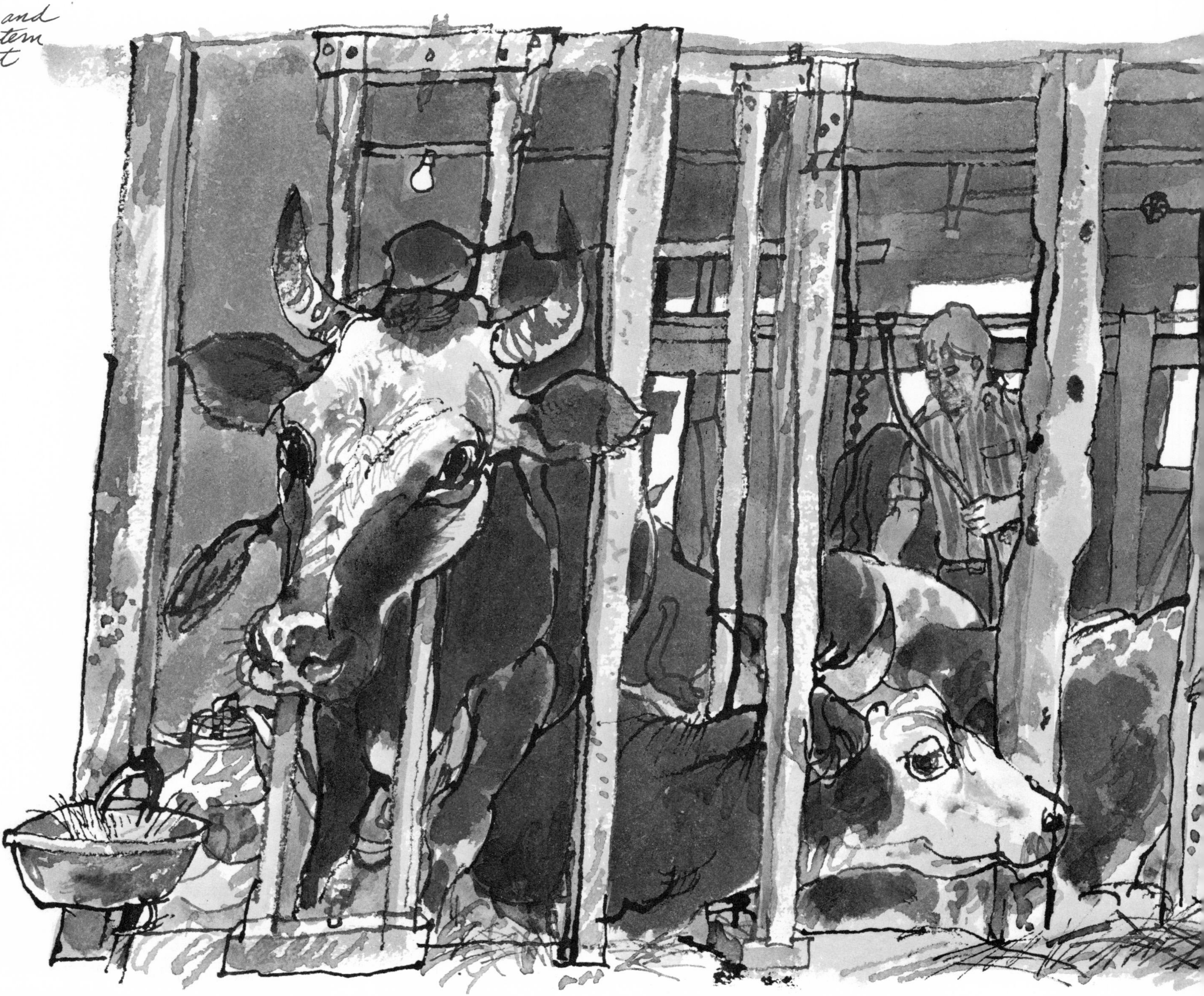

Road from Hardwick

John George's "Idle Hours Farm" on the Mackville Road offers very few idle hours for this farmer. Taking care of his beloved cows takes all of his time. I sketched and he spoke personally to each cow as he placed the milkers or removed them.

The one-day-old calf doing the licking in the picture never seemed to tire of this occupation. Even the kitten got lapped.

John George's "Idle Hours Farm", near Hardwick

Marway Farm near Hardwick

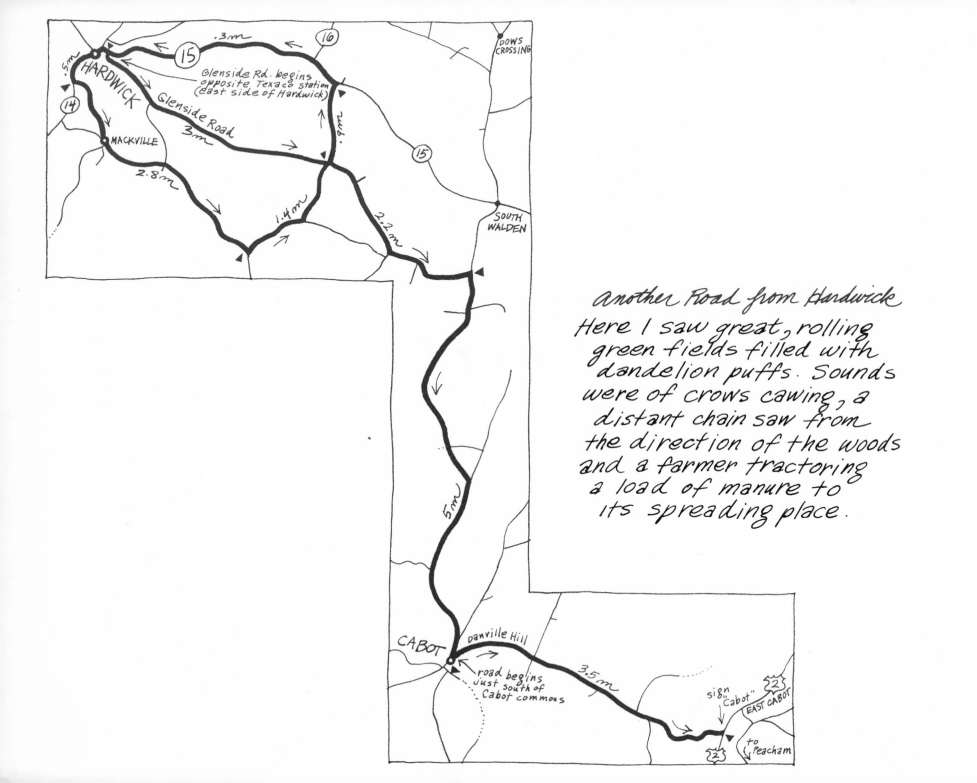

.3m

15

16

5m

.5m

HARDWICK

14

Glenside Rd. begins
opposite Texaco station
(east side of Hardwick)

Glenside Road

3m

MACKVILLE

.9m

15

2.8m

1.4m

2.2m

DOWS
CROSSING

SOUTH
WALDEN

5m

CABOT

Danville Hill

road begins
just south of
Cabot commons

3.5m

sign
"Cabot"

2

EAST CABOT

2

to
Peacham

Another Road from Hardwick

Here I saw great, rolling
green fields filled with
dandelion puffs. Sounds
were of crows cawing, a
distant chain saw from
the direction of the woods
and a farmer tractoring
a load of manure to
its spreading place.

Peacham and Danville Roads

Church bells chimed a melody at halfpast the hour out over quiet Peacham village.

From Peacham, just above South Danville, there is a neat, short covered bridge over rushing Joe's Brook.

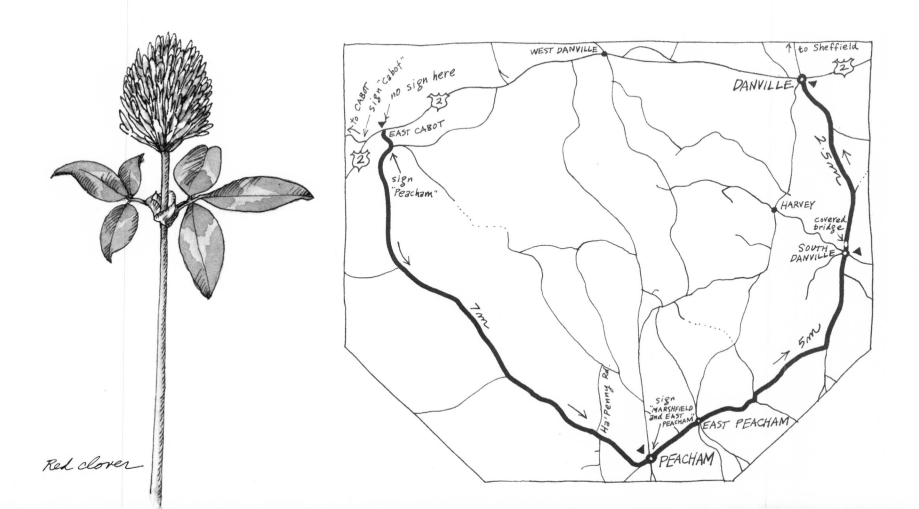

Red clover

Peacham

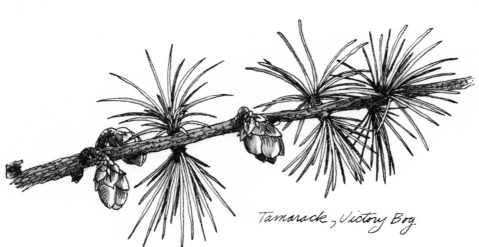

Tamarack, Victory Bog

North Concord to Sheffield to Danville

Here is a back road along the Moose River through the primitive flat landscape of Victory Bog, an area of little population. Leaving the river and going west toward Burke Hollow, the land becomes hilly again and farms reappear.

Front porch wash, West Burke

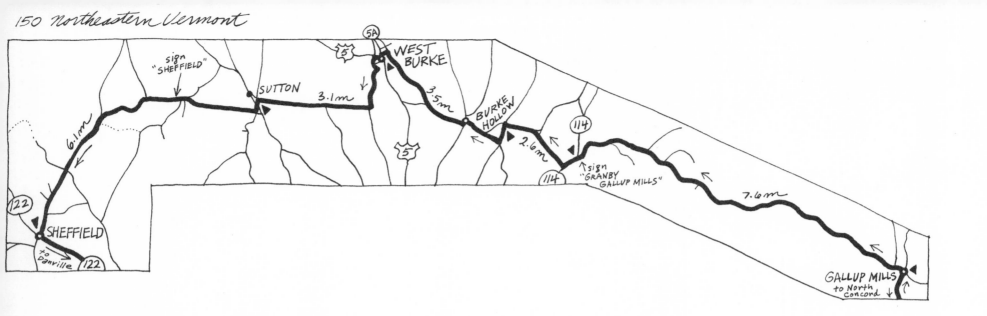

Robin Plantain

From West Burke to Sutton there is rolling farmland and some thick forest and then a picturesque view approaching Sheffield.

The postmistress told me that the town was "just a small farming community of people who cooperate with one another."

Sheffield

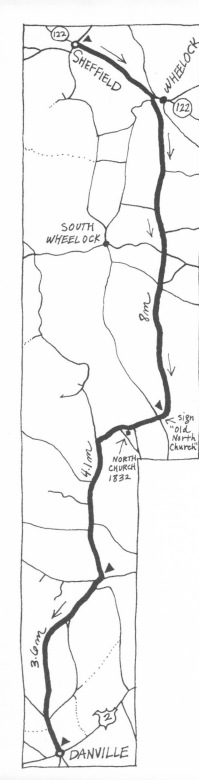

wild cherry

I reached Danville
as the postmaster was
lowering the flag
at the end
of day.

Danville

POST OFFICE
DANVILLE

New Hampshire

Northern New Hampshire is an area of massive mountains. There are few back roads branching off into those precipitous chasms. Adjacent to the mountains however, as in Vermont, back roads are delightful to travel and you may experience joy in the beauty of the landscape.

Blue Flag

LISBON
SUGAR HILL
BATH
EASTON
WENTWORTH
ELLSWORTH   CONWAY
WEST
CAMPTON   EAST MADISON
WEST   EFFINGHAM
RUMNEY   RUMNEY   FALLS
CHEEVER
                              TUFTONBORO
GROTON   OSSIPEE
HEBRON   CENTER
                     TUFTONBORO

BELMONT
                    GILMANTON
LOWER   IRONWORKS
GILMANTON
SHAKER   CENTER
VILLAGE   BARNSTEAD
      EAST
      CONCORD

New Hampshire

Back Road to Lisbon

The back road to Lisbon offers
a long view of the town
     across the Ammonoosuc
River. Just before crossing the
bridge there's a lawn and
     benches, a place to sketch
and to listen to the roar of
the falls. The town was once
     known as Concord, then
Chiswick, followed by Gunthwaite;
     however, in 1824 it became
Lisbon after the great
     Portuguese city. Saying
"Liz-bon" slowly sounds good
     and vibrates the tongue
and brain, I discovered.

Ammonoosuc River at Lisbon

Klay Knoll Farm, Bath

The Road to Bath

I tried to include as much as I could of 600-acre Klay Knoll Farm. Farmer Lester Presby is pictured three times, first emerging on the right as he started his tractor, later on climbing the road on the left to spread some manure, then finally in the foreground "teddering" (turning the hay over to dry).

Enter Bath over the long covered bridge and see its fine brick buildings including the old country store.

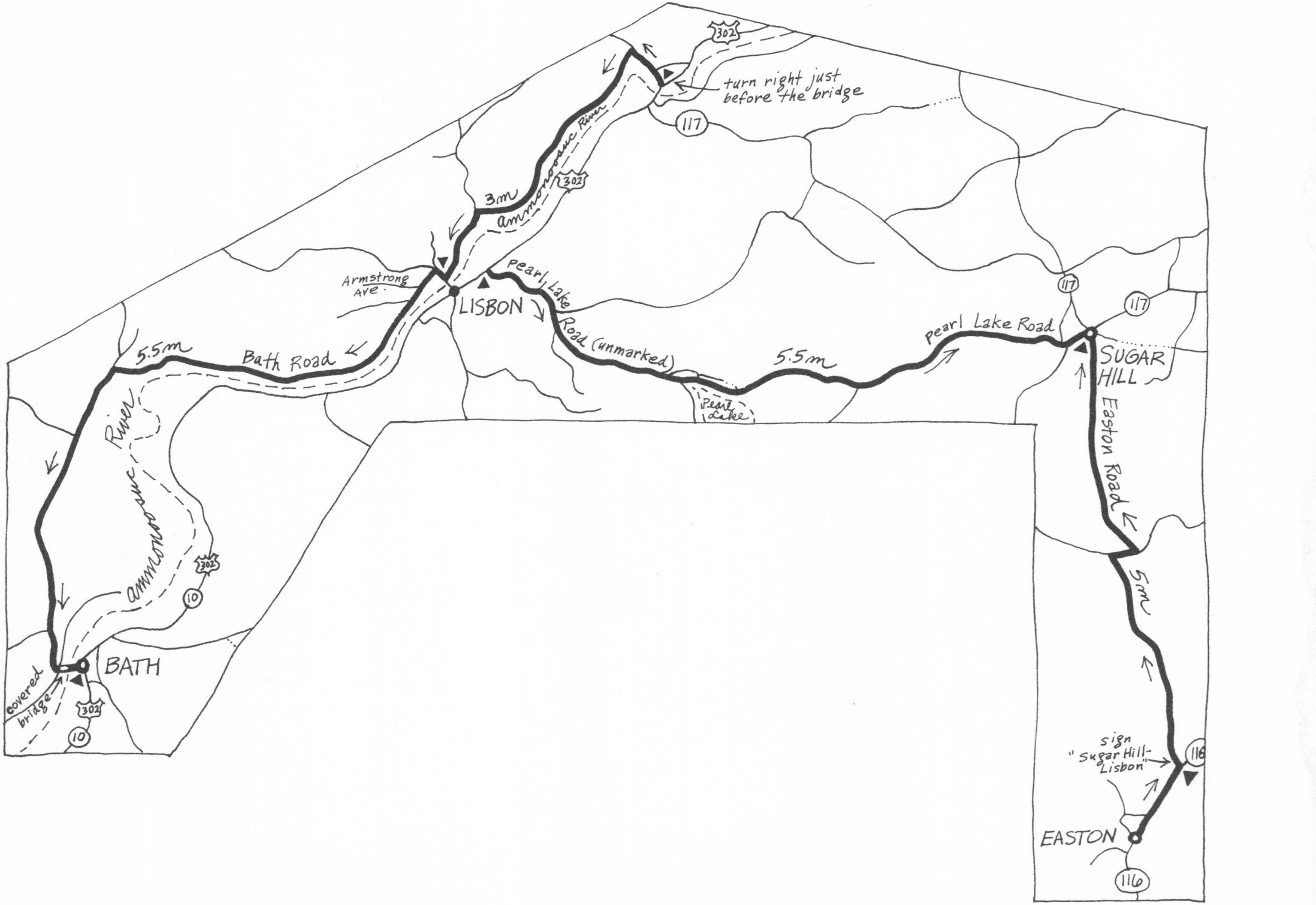

302

turn right just
before the bridge

117

3m

302

ammonoosuc River

Armstrong
Ave.

Pearl Lake

LISBON

117

117

Pearl Lake Road

SUGAR
HILL

5.5m

Bath Road

Pearl Lake Road (unmarked)

5.5m

River

ammonoosuc

302

10

Easton Road

5m

covered
bridge

BATH

302

10

sign
"Sugar Hill-
Lisbon"

116

EASTON

116

Lester Presby,
Klay Knoll Farm, Bath

Roads to Sugar Hill

These marvelous picture-inspiring roads begin in Lisbon and Easton. In Sugar Hill people remember the Sweetpea Farm when it actually sold sweetpeas to the many large summer hotels that once flourished in this area. Today the farm is a fine private home restored by the Jessemans. The left side was built in 1830, the right in 1887, the vintage car in 1929, I think.

Sweet Pea Farm, Sugar Hill

SWEET PEA FARM
THE D.E. JESSEMANS

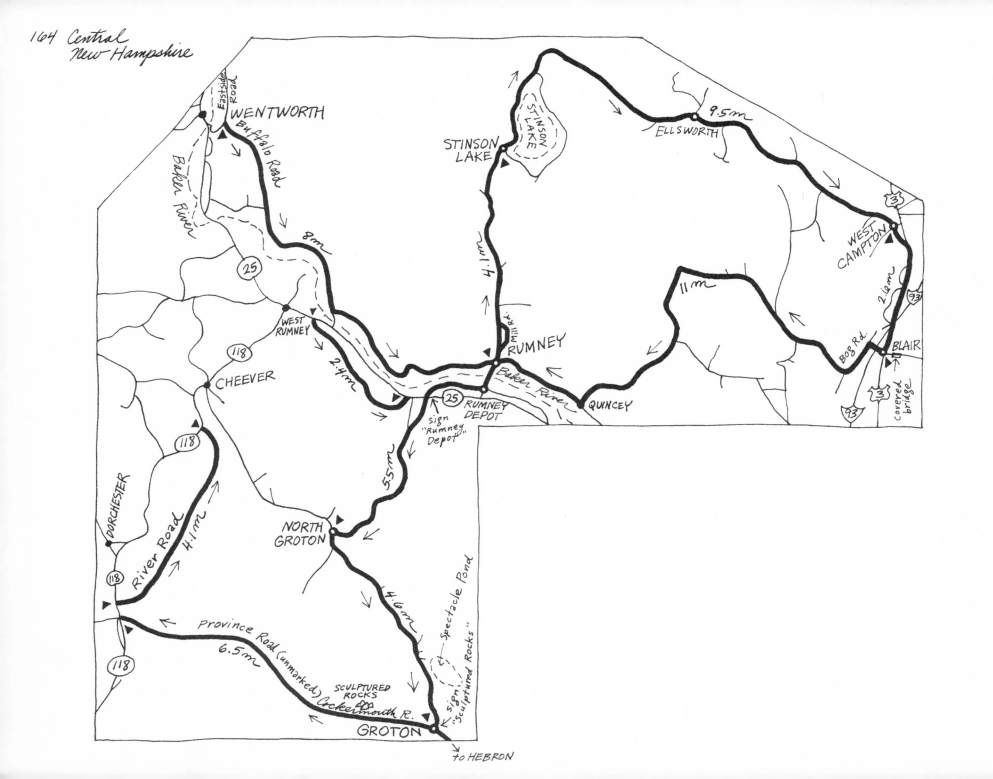

WENTWORTH

Eastside Road

Buffalo Road

Baker River

25

8m

WEST
RUMNEY

118

CHEEVER

2.4m

118

DORCHESTER

118

River Road

4.1m

118

5.5m

NORTH
GROTON

Province Road (unmarked)

6.5m

Crockermouth R.

SCULPTURED
ROCKS

GROTON

to HEBRON

sign
"Sculptured Rocks"

4.6m

Spectacle Pond

sign
"Rumney
Depot"

25

RUMNEY
DEPOT

Baker River

QUINCEY

RUMNEY

Millbrook

4.1m

STINSON
LAKE

STINSON
LAKE

ELLSWORTH

9.5m

3

WEST
CAMPTON

11m

2.6m

Bog Rd.

93

BLAIR

3

93

covered
bridge

Road Along the Cockermouth River

Past the picturesque village of Hebron and out of Groton is the geological masterpiece, "Sculptured Rocks", shaped through time by rushing, charging water. From here the road narrows and becomes more primitive. To me it was like proceeding through a hole in the forest, the beauty of the woods closer about me than on any other drive. This was the most adventurous of my back roads trips through New England.

Sculptured Rocks near Groton

Lupine

Wentworth to Rumney

The post office on the common in Wentworth has church notices in the window including a plea for the organ fund. There was also the following, "Piano Recitals by the pupils of Marcella Hoffman, Russell School, Rumney." Several cows grazed in the meadow behind the post office as I read each and every item.

Roads to Rumney

Along River Road, as in many places in New England, rock walls indicating old farm fields and boundaries vanish from view as brush and trees grow back.

In Rumney I sketched the former home of the founder of Christian Science, Mary Baker Eddy.

There are notable mountain views on the road past Stinson Lake to West Campton.

From Rumney, again, you climb toward North Groton with a churning river at your side.

Mary Baker Eddy house, Rumney

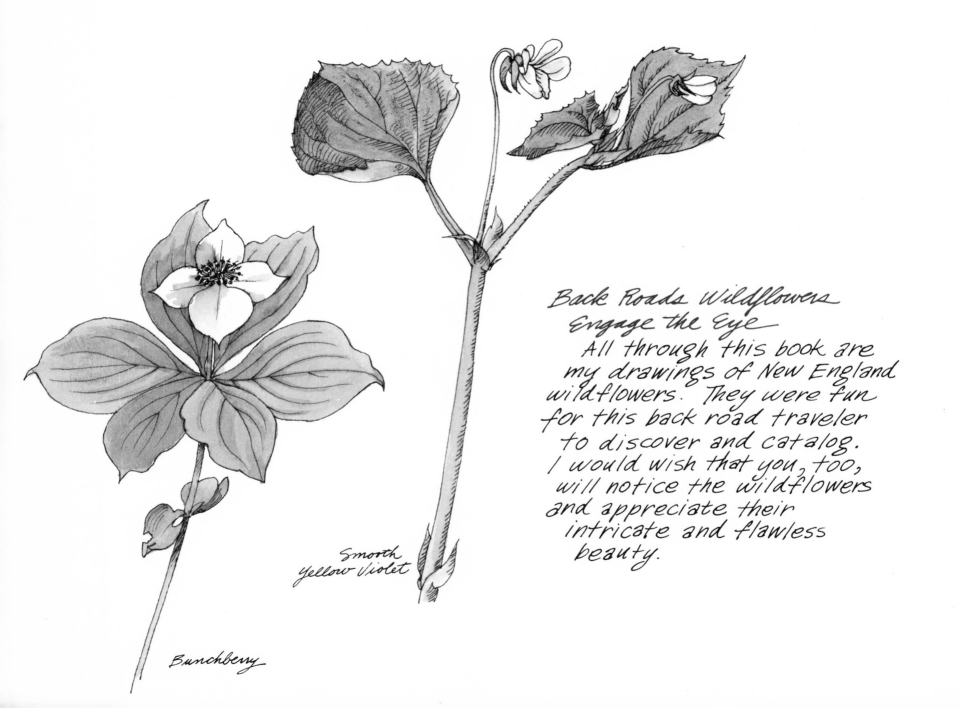

Smooth
Yellow Violet

Bunchberry

Back Roads Wildflowers
Engage the Eye
  All through this book are
  my drawings of New England
wildflowers. They were fun
for this back road traveler
  to discover and catalog.
I would wish that you, too,
  will notice the wildflowers
and appreciate their
    intricate and flawless
        beauty.

Hobblebush

False Solomon's Seal

Bladder Campion

The Road Past Shaker Village

It was only a few years ago that the Paul Revere bell was re-identified in the belfry of the old Dwelling House at Shaker Village. This building was chapel and dining hall for the Shaker religious sect in 1825. The road past Shaker Village from Concord ends among the handsome white homes of Belmont town.

The Dwelling House,
Shaker Village

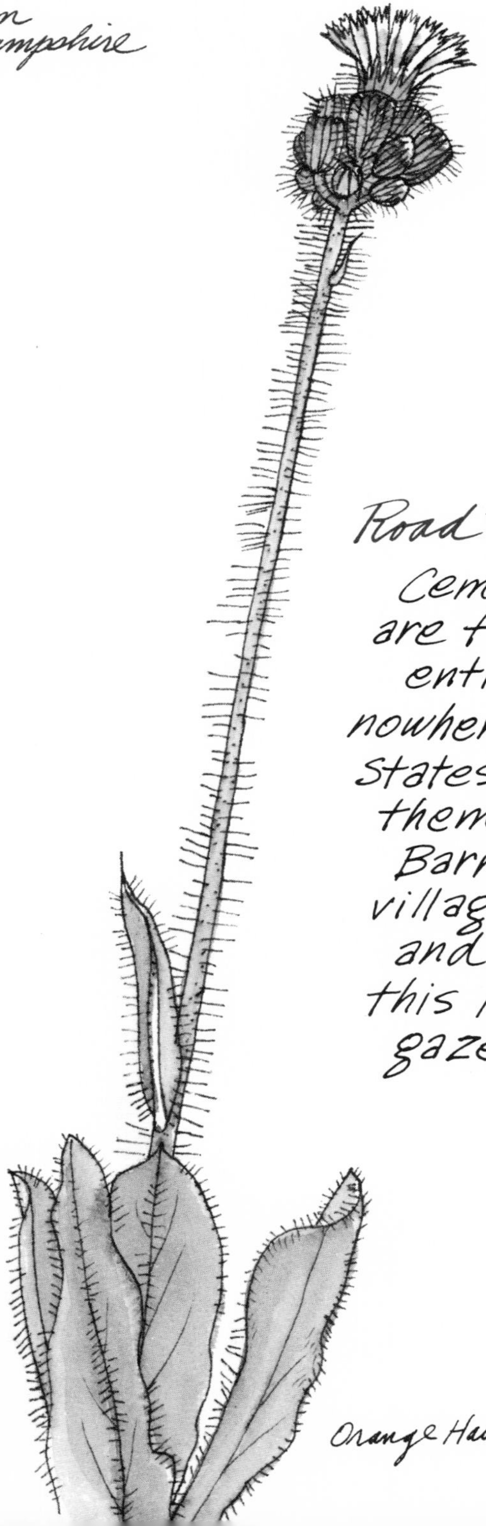

Road to Gilmanton Ironworks

 Cemeteries in New England
are fascinating sculptural
entities. And, perhaps
nowhere else in these United
States are there so many of
them. The road from Center
Barnstead to the hillside
village of Gilmanton Ironworks
and Crystal Lake passes
this little cemetery with the
gazebo in the center.

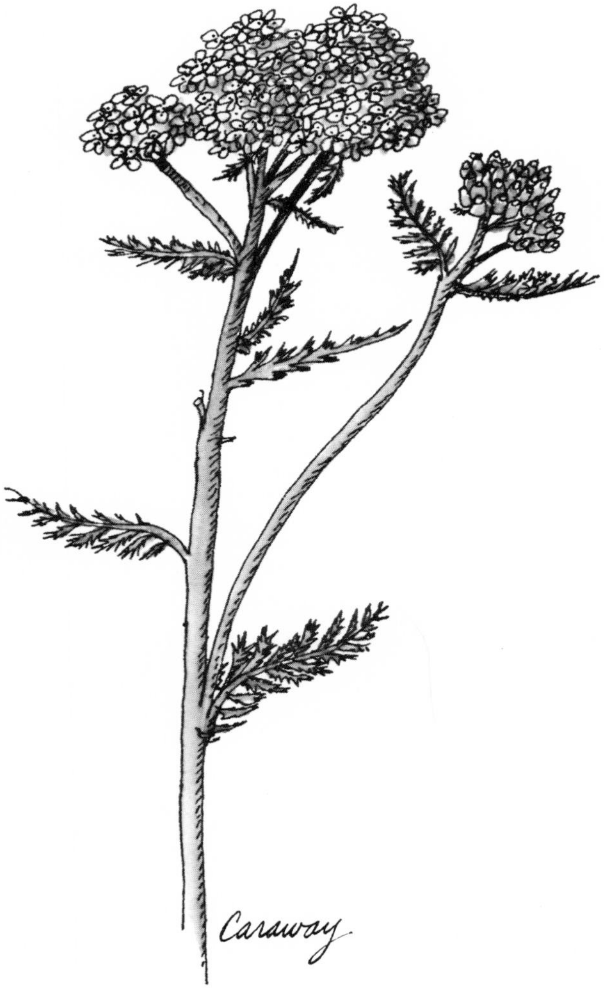

Caraway.

Orange Hawkweed

Gilmanton Ironworks cemetery

Road to Center Barnstead

The church at Center
Barnstead has an old-
fashioned interior with a
great, low, hanging
chandelier. Pews face the
front door, to the dismay
of those who find
themselves late for
service and must face
the entire congregation
while proceeding to
their seats.

The Soldier and Sailor
Memorial in front of the
church is in memory of
those who died in the
wars of 1776-83, 1812-14,
1846-48, 1861-65 and
1917-19. Flags flying
from many a gravesite
and memorial are
placed by the
American Legion.

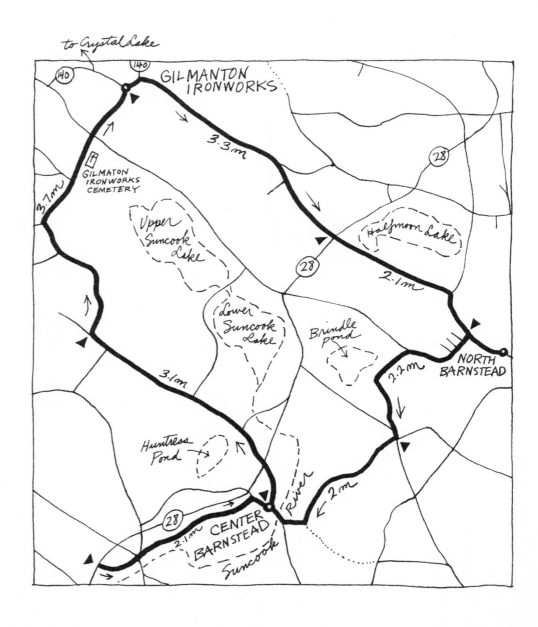

Center Barnstead

Two Roads to Ossipee

From Center Tuftonboro or farther east from North Wakefield good country roads lead to Ossipee.

The Walter White house in Ossipee has many additions. Originally the main house was a small "Cape-Codder," vintage 1850. It was then raised up one story and the barn to the left added. The elevated porch provided the occupants a place to sit and watch the carriages go by. The addition on the right was once a millinery shop, then a restaurant, and now is part of the main house. The latest addition, in 1952, is the garage on the left with an elephant weathervane celebrating Eisenhower's election to the presidency.

A house in Ossipee

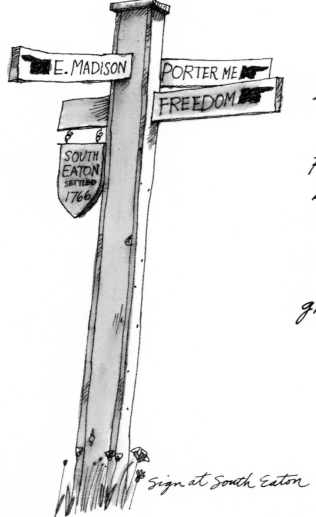

E. MADISON

PORTER ME

FREEDOM

SOUTH EATON SETTLED 1766

Sign at South Eaton

Backroad through Effingham Falls
to East Madison

The Davis barn near Effingham
Falls sits solidly on great granite
blocks, cut and fitted neatly to form
a permanent base for the heavily
timbered barn. Some pillars inside
on the ground floor are also
granite. Part of the original
granite corral is on the other
side of the barn.

The Davis Farm near Effingham town

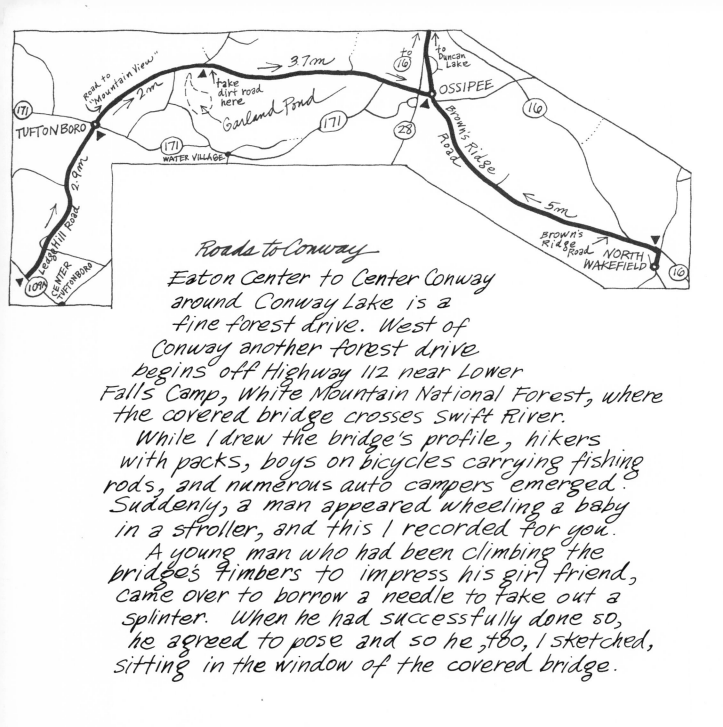

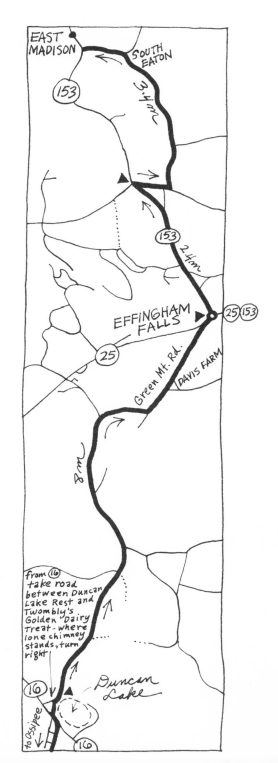

Roads to Conway

Eaton Center to Center Conway
around Conway Lake is a
fine forest drive. West of
Conway another forest drive
begins off Highway 112 near Lower
Falls Camp, White Mountain National Forest, where
the covered bridge crosses Swift River.

While I drew the bridge's profile, hikers
with packs, boys on bicycles carrying fishing
rods, and numerous auto campers emerged.
Suddenly, a man appeared wheeling a baby
in a stroller, and this I recorded for you.

A young man who had been climbing the
bridge's timbers to impress his girl friend,
came over to borrow a needle to take out a
splinter. When he had successfully done so,
he agreed to pose and so he, too, I sketched,
sitting in the window of the covered bridge.

Map labels (left map):
171 TUFTONBORO
Road to "Mountain View"
3.7m
2m
take dirt road here
Garland Pond
171
WATER VILLAGE
171
Leg & Hill Road 2.9m
CENTER TUFTONBORO
109A
to 16
to Duncan Lake
16
OSSIPEE
16
28
Brown's Ridge Road
5m
Brown's Ridge Road
NORTH WAKEFIELD
16

Map labels (right map):
EAST MADISON
SOUTH EATON
153
3.4m
153
2.4m
EFFINGHAM FALLS
25 153
25
Green Mt. Rd.
DAVIS FARM
8m
from 16 take road between Duncan Lake Rest and Twombly's Golden Dairy Treat- where lone chimney stands, turn right
16
Duncan Lake
to Ossipee
16

Bridge over the Swift River, near Conway

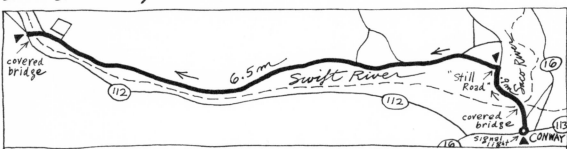

Dwarf Cinquefoil

meadow Rue

Maine

The large state of Maine gives one
the feeling of being completely
engulfed by forests. After
traveling the interior back
roads through hundreds of
miles of beautiful woods and
lakes I felt a longing to see
the coast and the ocean.
The northern coast of Maine
was my area of exploration.

BAXTER
STATE
PARK

•KOKADJO

MILLINOCKET•

GREENVILLE•

Maine

CALAIS•

LUBEC•

ANSON
•STARKS
NEW SHARON
•VIENNA
•MT. VERNON

QUODDY
HEAD
SOUTH TRESCOTT•
NORTH CUTLER•
CUTLER•

•ADDISON
JONESPORT•

•READFIED
•LOCKE MILLS •WAYNE
LEEDS•

HANCOCK POINT
WINTER
HARBOR

•NORTH MONMOUTH

BUCKFIELD•
PARIS•

DEER ISLE•
STONINGTON•

South Pond to
Pennesseewasee Lake

The road from Locke Mills
hugged South Pond for
several miles. The
pond's surface
was unruffled and
the water appeared
dark and mysterious.
There are three
more ponds along
this road before
one reaches the
big Pennesseewasee.

Road along South Pond near Locke Mills

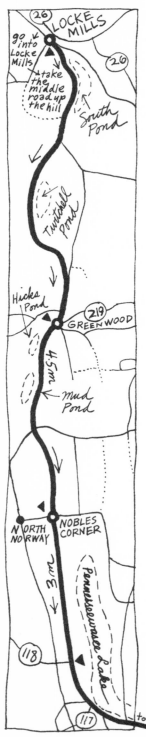

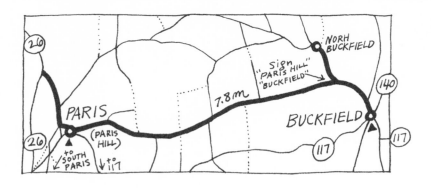

Road to Paris

The stone jail on the Paris common is built with huge blocks of granite. An X marks the spot on the outside where a stone was successfully removed by an escapee. The stone was replaced and fastened over the spot to insure against this happening again. That was a long time ago, for the jail has been the Paris Library since 1900. Hannibal Hamlin, vice president to Lincoln, lived in the house just north of the jail and the view from here toward the White Mountains of New Hampshire is quite dramatic. Paris, or Paris Hill as it is also called, evokes the atmosphere of another age.

The stone jail, Paris

Paris to Buckfield

On the road to North Buckfield I sketched this mailbox arrangement. The farmer had an old post he thought he'd put to use, he told me, and the wire pulling the chain is meant to keep the mailbox out of the way of the snowplow come winter.

mail rig, Buckfield

Snow flag, Paris

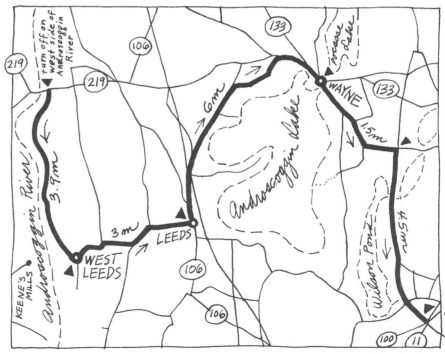

219

turn off on
west side of
Androscoggin
River

106

133

219

Moose Lake

WAYNE

133

6m

Androscoggin Lake

1.5m

Androscoggin River

3.9m

KEENE'S
MILLS

3m

LEEDS

WEST
LEEDS

106

106

106

4.5m

Wilson Pond

NORTH
MONMOUTH

100

11

ANNABESSACOOK

Golden Alexander

North Monmouth and the Androscoggin

This trip meanders along the Androscoggin River to the tiny community of West Leeds, then past Androscoggin Lake and Wilson Pond. At North Monmouth Moncena Burnham had created a water-powered miniature carnival with dolls as participants. At night the display continued with colored lights revolving along with the dolls in gay carnival fashion.

miniature carnival by water power,
North Monmouth

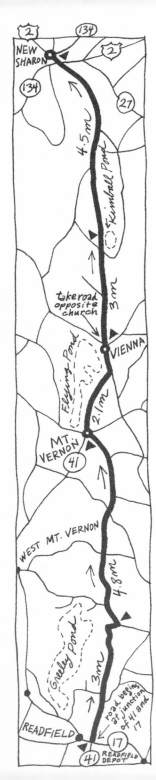

Readfield to
New Sharon

From Readfield
a country road
goes past
farmhouses,
meadows, some
forest, three
cemeteries, rock
walls, and, finally,
down to Mt. Vernon
on Minnehonk Pond.
Carriage builders
once worked here and
there used to be a
gristmill.
   A little farther
north is the neat
village of Vienna
(pronounced "Vy-enna").
   A primitive road past
Kimball Pond goes on to
New Sharon; however you
must ask locally about the
condition of the road.

Mt. Vernon

New Sharon once had a covered
bridge. Jed Grant, proprietor
of the country store, showed
me photographs of the early
1900s floods that had
washed it away.

New Sharon

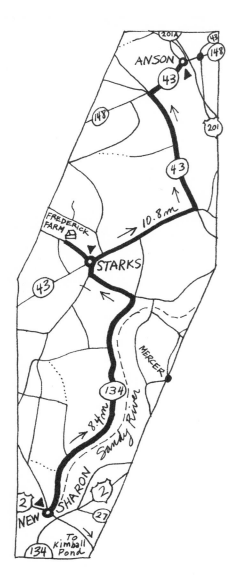

The covered bridge was replaced in 1916 by the steel one you see in my drawing. In the 50s a new bridge bypassed it. The old one is still used but is closed to lumber trucks and school buses. Ride over it. There is no danger, I'm sure, but with the Sandy River far below there is the feeling that one should really hurry a bit to the safety of the opposite bank.

New Sharon to Starks

The Frederick Farm is about a mile north of the sleepy town of Starks. Five generations of this family of farmers are buried in the cemetery on the nearby hill.

Mr. Frederick told me, "Painting pictures come natural. That I could never do. Milking cows, now, that I can do. Been milking cows for fifty years and that come natural to me!"   The Frederick sons are not farmers, so the hard work of carrying on the family farm may end with this older generation.

The Frederick Farm, Starks

Greenville to Millinocket

This longest back road in the book goes about 70 miles through both public and private lands. Some 15 miles past Lily Bay is a point where you record for private landholders where you are from and what your purpose is. "Riding" was mine.

I sketched Baxter State Park's Mount Katahdin, the bit of United States territory, it was claimed, that receives the first light of the sun each morning. Percival Baxter, former governor of Maine, purchased and gave this land to Maine, saying, "Man is born to die, his works are short-lived, buildings crumble, monuments decay, wealth vanishes, but Katahdin shall remain— the mountain of the people of Maine."

Mt. Katahdin

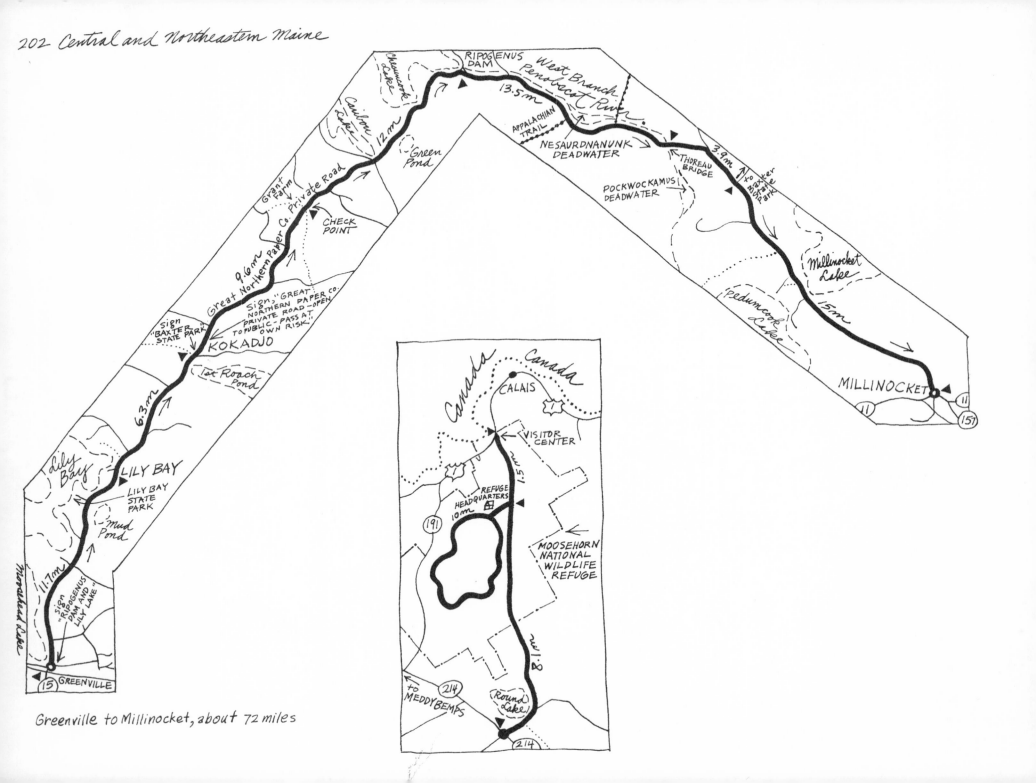

Chaumcook Lake

Caribou Lake

RIPOGENUS DAM

West Branch Penobscot River

13.5 m

APPALACHIAN TRAIL

NESAURDNANUNK DEADWATER

THOREAU BRIDGE

3.9 m

to Baxter State Park

POCKWOCKAMUS DEADWATER

12 m

Green Pond

Grant Farm

Great Northern Paper Co. Private Road

CHECK POINT

9.6 m

Sign "GREAT NORTHERN PAPER CO. PRIVATE ROAD—OPEN TO PUBLIC—PASS AT OWN RISK"

Sign "BAXTER STATE PARK"

KOKADJO

1st Roach Pond

Millinocket Lake

Pedumcook Lake

15 m

6.3 m

Lily Bay

LILY BAY

LILY BAY STATE PARK

Mud Pond

11.7 m

Sign "RIPOGENUS DAM AND LILY LAKE"

Moosehead Lake

15 GREENVILLE

MILLINOCKET

11

157

Greenville to Millinocket, about 72 miles

Canada   Canada

CALAIS

VISITOR CENTER

1.5 m

REFUGE HEADQUARTERS

10 m

191

MOOSEHORN NATIONAL WILDLIFE REFUGE

8.1 m

to MEDDYBEMPS

214

Round Lake

214

Columbine

Moosehorn Back Road

There are twelve stops on this 10-mile trip and mimeographed sheets you pick up at the entrance give information about each stop.

I sketched Fire Pond at stop #7 to the twanging sounds and gutteral burps of frogs. My instructions read, "The standing dead timber attracts the insects, the main diet of young ducks. As trees fall down the logs are used as loafing sites where the ducks may preen their colorful feathers."

Fire Pond, Moosehorn National Wildlife Refuge

Ox-eye Daisy

From Lubec

Near the Canadian border, on the ocean, is Lubec. The tide was out and the fog thick in the hilly, picturesque, fishing village as I sketched old Pike's Wharf. Although International Bridge to Campobello Island was in the background it was lost from view. Franklin Delano Roosevelt would visit Campobello by taking the boat from Eastport, but now you can visit his old summer home by merely crossing the auto bridge at Lubec.

Pike's Wharf, Lubec

Quoddy Head and South

At the fog-bound easternmost piece of
United States territory the horns were
trumpeting their deafening, bone-jarring
warnings. The Coast Guard man in charge
said that he is so used to the sound
that, when indoors, he forgets it
entirely. A lobster boat
maneuvered offshore in the fog,
dangerously close, it seemed
to me, to the treacherous
rocky shore.

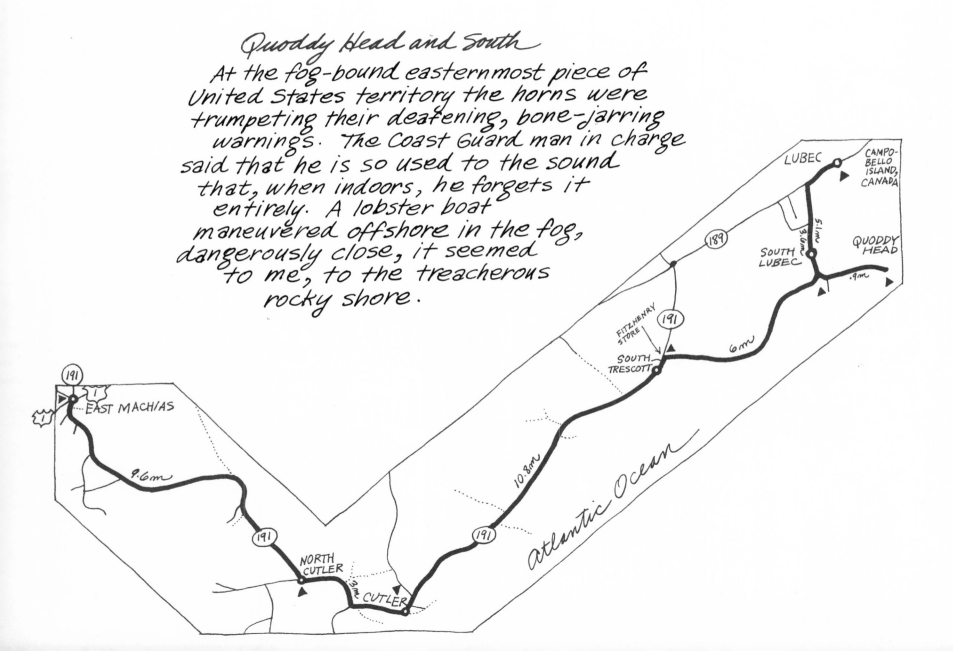

LUBEC

CAMPO-
BELLO
ISLAND,
CANADA

5.1m

3.0m

189

SOUTH
LUBEC

QUODDY
HEAD

.9m

FITZHENRY
STORE

191

6m

SOUTH
TRESCOTT

191

191

EAST MACHIAS

1

1

9.6m

10.8m

Atlantic Ocean

NORTH
CUTLER

.3m

CUTLER

191

Quoddy Head Light Station

Mrs. Moore's clotheslines, Trescott

The Road to Cutler

    Mrs. Moore has all the room she needs for colorful clotheslines. One line, filled with the wash of her seven children, stretched clear out of my picture into the nearby woods.

From Cutler

Mr. Farris is a lobster
dealer and this is his
wharf. The wharf has
to accommodate a tide
of 13 feet. There
used to be more
wharfs and double the
population here in Cutler
in the 1930s when fishing
favored the smaller
fisherman in business.
Now it is only lobsters,
for the most part,
that Farris deals in. The
boat tied to the
wharf is one he uses
to fetch lobsters from
lobstermen up and
down the coast in the
more remote areas.

The Road to Jonesport

A Victorian dwelling of multipatterned shingling,
 the Sawyer house sits prominently by the
bay with Beal's Island in the background.
 A marina is now being built nearby, a place
 for small pleasure boats and yachts to stop,
evidence of the area's change from fishing
 to tourism as a source of income.
 Crossing Moosabec Reach on Bridge Street
 there are roads to explore on Beal's and
 Great Wass Island near Jonesport.

The Sawyer House, 1895,
 Jonesport

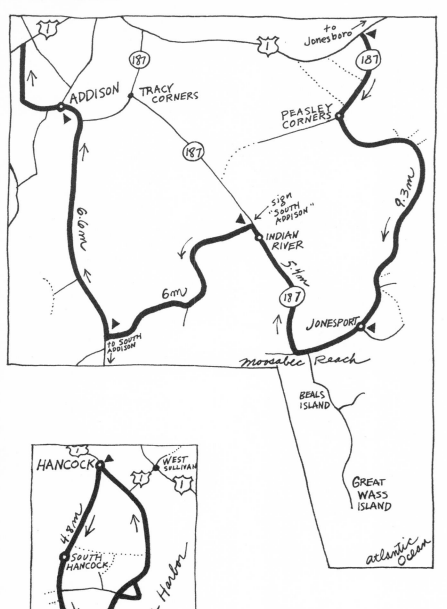

Roads around Hancock

Hancock Point has splendid summer homes nestled among trees and along the shore. The road to Carter's Beach ended on the beach contrary to the map information I had. Views from shore are of many islands and peninsulas.

Carter's Beach
Hancock Point

Mark and Ned Islands

Road around Schoodic

The road is one way from Winter Harbor around Schoodic Peninsula and emerging at Birch Harbor. Schoodic is part of Acadia National Park and is famous for its crashing surf.
My sketch looks toward Mark and Ned, islands that connect at low tide.

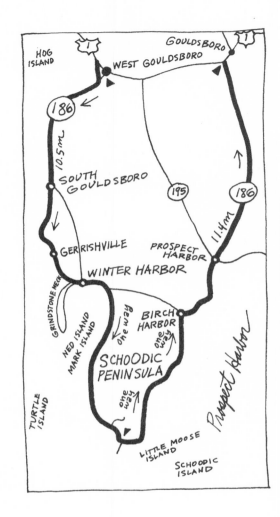

Stonington

Road to Stonington

The landscape is rolling and beautiful as you drive past tiny harbors and bays. At Stonington I drew a pink granite piece of shore with lobster boats and fishing shacks. I conversed with a young lobster fisherman who gets up at 5 in the morning and home again from the sea at 3 in the afternoon. I asked him if he liked lobstering. "You get used to it," was his reply.

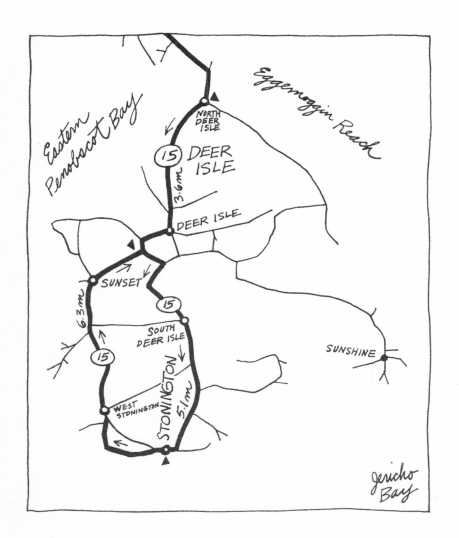

Eastern
Penobscot Bay

Eggemoggin Reach

NORTH
DEER
ISLE

⑮ DEER
ISLE

3.6 m

DEER ISLE

SUNSET

⑮

6.3 m

SOUTH
DEER ISLE

SUNSHINE

⑮

STONINGTON

5.1 m

WEST
STONINGTON

Jericho
Bay

WESTERN AVE.

street sign, Jonesport

Epilogue

I wish you to hear the forest and farm sounds, the bird choruses, feel the rocks and the grass, enjoy the spring green, the fall color, and experience the proud heritage of early America through seeing the many historic places in New England.

I hope you will make it your plan when you ride the back roads to greet people in friendliness and trust and to take an interest in their way of living.

I urge you to support efforts to protect nature and to preserve structures that express our heritage. This includes steps to improve the automobile, to the point where it no longer is an instrument of pollution. Resist "progress" where it endangers beauty and health and the preservation of historical sites.

The needs of planet earth must now supercede those of mankind, I truly believe.

Earl Thollander

young deer

A bamboo pen, fashioned by myself, was used for most of the drawings in this book. Black, waterproof ink was my medium, along with a bottle of diluted ink for grey tones. An Esterbrook fountain pen with a flexible point and black water-soluble fountain pen ink was used for the other, more delicate sketches. Sable hair brushes were employed for washes. The paper used was Fabriano Classico watercolor paper 140 pound rough for bamboo pen work and Classico 140 pound hot press for fountain pen drawings. All drawings were completed on location.